WELCOME

LAND ROVERS can justifiably claim to be the world's most influential 4x4 having inspired their owners to travel with them, modify them, rebuild them and go adventuring with them. Over almost 60 years of manufacture, Land Rovers have been relied on for everyday transport, and for all-weather weekend cars. They may be battered and bent or bright and shiny, as smooth as sewing machines or as rough as a bag of rusty nails, but whatever condition they're in it's guaranteed that their owners will be lavishing mountains of time, effort and money on their upkeep.

A Land Rover is for life and it inspires each and every owner to go that little bit further, put in that little bit of extra effort, become resourceful, patient and innovative. In short a Land Rover can take over your life.

LAND ROVER *monthly* has been reporting on the Land Rover scene since 1998 and in that time we have so often become inspired ourselves by the stories that have featured in our pages. In this book we've brought together some of our favourites and I'm sure that you will find them as enjoyable and inspirational as we have.

Wherever there's a Land Rover there's a story to tell – it might be modifications to meet the strains and stresses of 'winch challenge' competitions, or a gentle rebuild of a Range Rover to its former grand magnificence. It might be an exciting drive in a brand new Discovery, or a desert expedition on a shoestring in a beat up old Series One. You name it and a Land Rover has done it.

If all that inspires you to buy your first Land Rover or maybe trade up to a newer version, then we've also included here some hints and suggestions to help you make the right decision.

Enjoy the book and I hope that the inspiration behind the vehicles on these pages rubs off and leaves you wanting to get out there right away with your own Land Rover.

Richard Howell Thomas
Editor, **LAND ROVER** *monthly*

LAND ROVER
THE INSPIRATIONAL 4x4

Compiled by
Richard Howell Thomas

With special thanks to
David Bowers Andy Cutting
Nick Dimbleby Andy Egerton
John Henderson Jenny Morgan
Bob Morrison Les Roberts
Ash Sweeting
Cathie Howell Thomas
Daniel Hunt Ellie Baskett
Nick King

© 2␣␣␣␣␣␣␣␣␣␣␣␣␣␣␣␣␣␣␣␣␣␣␣␣Ltd

ISBN 978-0-9552013-0-1

golden gate

INSPIRED TO REBUILD

INSPIRED TO MODIFY

INSPIRED TO TRAVEL

CONTENTS

INSPIRED TO DRIVE

INSPIRED TO OWN/BUY

WITH ALMOST a third of a million miles on the clock, and an exemplary reliability record to boot, this 1971 Range Rover underlines the long-term durability of these vehicles and John Edwins, who lives in Stanbridge, near Leighton Buzzard, has only one outstanding criticism. After 26 years in his ownership, the engine finally gave up the ghost after covering 255,000 miles.

Judging by the Range Rover's present day condition, it would be easy to assume that it's led a pampered life, but this is not so. John is a painter and decorator by trade and, in its earlier years, it was

Words and pictures
David Bowers

John Edwins' beautifully restored pride and joy – a 1971 Range Rover with almost a third of a million miles on the clock.

used to ferry around a gang of workers, heavy tools and bags of cement. Recreational use has involved off-roading, both of the normal four-wheel variety and following sets of hoof tracks across the countryside, as John explains.

hoof tracks

"I used to take the Range Rover down to the chalk pits near where I live for some off-roading, where it could do things that you couldn't do on foot without falling over or dare to attempt in any other kind of vehicle. My wife rode with the local hunt at the time, the Aldenham

Harriers, and I used to follow the hunt in the Range Rover, which resulted in a few 'moments'. These vehicles will go through a hedge, but not over one and I ripped the front brake hydraulic hoses one day when I got a bit too carried away."

The Range Rover was soon mended and it also served the couple's interest in equestrian pursuits towing a twin-axle Rice double pony trailer to gymkhanas, pony racing events and transporting a two-wheeled trap – a Liverpool Lawton. John won the mascot on the Range Rover's bonnet in a bet with another racing

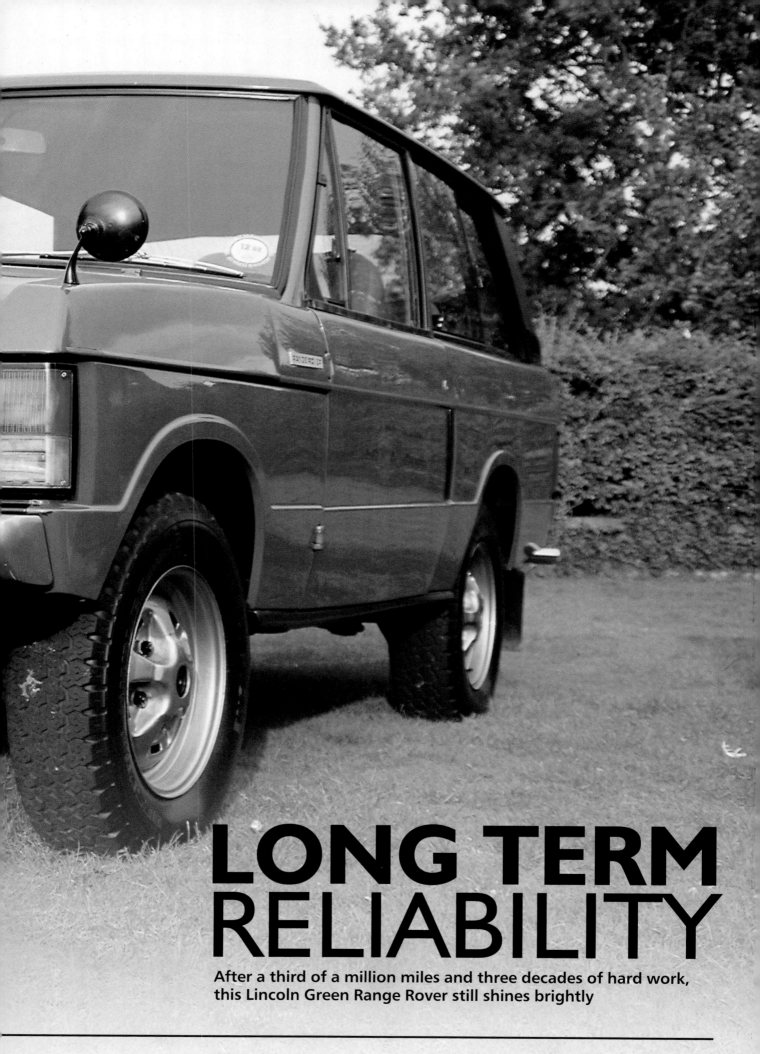

LONG TERM RELIABILITY

After a third of a million miles and three decades of hard work,
this Lincoln Green Range Rover still shines brightly

event contestant on whose horse would take the honours in what is known as a 'flapping' event, and it has been proudly displayed on every vehicle that he's subsequently owned.

These included his first Range Rover, a 1970 model, in Lincoln Green, which was reluctantly sold after a cash crisis, although John vowed he'd buy himself another when business picked up. In time it did and his present Range Rover was bought secondhand when it was four years old from Camden Motors of Leighton Buzzard.

As mentioned previously, the engine self-destructed at 255,000 miles due to the crowns of two pistons disintegrating pressurising the crankcase forcing the engine oil out of the block, leaving John stranded in deepest Devon. John was particularly downhearted, as he had only just collected the vehicle from a garage following a service that went disastrously wrong resulting in extensive damage to the four-speed manual gearbox.

"They put the Range Rover on a rolling road to test out the brakes and then set it running. The mechanic must have been very inex-

Above left: This Range Rover regularly tows John's ponies to driving events.
Top right: Deep pile carpets and cloth seats replaced the original plastic.
Above right: Fitting Monroe adjustable air dampers on the rear axle allows the ride height to be jacked up by three-inches.
Below: Removing rust from the footwells and rear wings formed a major part of the restoration.

perienced, as he decided to apply the handbrake, which acts as a transmission brake on the propshaft, of course, and this had very dire results for the gearbox", says John.

"I later spoke to a service engineer from Land Rover and he said that this bloke was lucky to be alive. Pulling on the handbrake when running at speed on a rolling road can throw these vehicles three feet into the air". The gearbox was repaired free of charge, which was just as well considering the outlay on a replacement factory engine was a major item of expenditure that left John reeling for a few months.

Other work undertaken prior to the restoration included fitting Monroe adjustable air dampers on the rear axle allowing the ride height to be jacked up by three-inches when required by means of a valve. This came in handy when transporting materials from site to site or when the vehicle was used to tow heavy trailers.

tedious but essential
John also owns a Jensen Interceptor Mark 1 that's been restored and is generally regarded as one of the best, if not the best, in the country.

So when the project on the Range Rover started in August 1994, he drew together the same team of professionals who had assisted him with the work on the Jensen. Steve Hughes of Dunstable did the welding and Terry Taylor of Leighton Buzzard did the respray. This left John with all those tedious but essential jobs, like stripping the paint off the bonnet, for example, which took all of a day and a half.

Removing all of the body panels from the rear of the 'A' post and down to the chassis revealed plenty of rust with the rear wheelarches and rear inner wings similarly affected. Steve Hughes carried out the necessary welding repairs which included letting in repair sections along the front edge of the floor pan. John then applied four coats of paint and two of Waxoyl to the inner wings. He also

doused the inside of the new tailgate with a liberal amount of Waxoyl, as these are so susceptible to rust, and also to any other nooks and crannies in the body that could potentially harbour moisture from water thrown up from the road surface.

bodyshop short cut

Fitting new sills was the first task and John was annoyed when he found out that, even though this had been done some years previously by a bodyshop, the replacements had been cut short at the back to avoid replacing the sill ends – a tricky job on a Range Rover and a short cut that had added to the rust problem. John had a set of sills made up by a friend, Mark Smith, a Range Rover specialist who trades from Borstal near Brill, Oxfordshire. Mark also supplied new inner and outer rear quarter panels. Attention was not required to the outer and inner front wings, as these had already been replaced.

The removal of the roof exposed corrosion along the top edge of the steel roof support panel that extends along the top of the wind-screen. The support panel was repaired after the area affected by rust had been cut out by welding-in a hand fabricated repair panel. The roof was then resprayed before being reattached – which turned out to be challenging in a seasonally improbable snowstorm during late spring – with no less than fifty self-tapping screws, a fiddly job at the best of times.

tough and lustrous

The respray involved the application of etch-primer and two-pack primer followed by coats of matt Lincoln Green, finally finished off by applica-tions of lacquer providing a tough and lustrous finish. The wheels and bumpers were sandblasted to bare metal and painted in two-pack silver.

John wasn't keen on the original

Top left: New tailgate was thoroughly soaked with Waxoyl.
Above left: Replacement engine – the original died at 250,000 miles.
Top right: "A vehicle that you can drive through a field... and then turn up at a five-star hotel..."
Below: Stripping off all the rear body panels revealed copious quanti-ties of rust.

specification plastic seats so he contacted a car upholstery firm who provided cloth seats on an exchange basis for the originals together with matching door and interior panels. A set of expensive, deep pile carpets provided the finishing touch – and woe betide anyone who gets in wearing dirty wellies.

As is so often the case, fitting a new headlining can cause more heartache than can be imagined for what appears to be a relatively easy task. "When I picked up the head-lining, I was advised not to try and fit it myself, to which I laughed because, on the face of it, the job seemed to be so easy," says John. "I wasn't laughing after struggling for five hours to get it into place. It was the most poxy job of them all. What a nightmare."

▶

The substitution of a five-speed gearbox had been considered when these first became available, although, after taking the long view, John had decided it wasn't worth the effort or expense at the time, as it would have taken twenty years to get the money back on reduced petrol expenditure. He also deliberated on whether to install power assisted steering, but abandoned the idea on the grounds that this would result in a loss of control and feel through the steering when off-roading.

The final mechanical tasks included fitting new front axle ball joints, new coil springs all round, a new brake servo, overhauling the brakes all round, fitting copper brake lines, and a new alternator.

accepted anywhere

John provides a resumé of what has endeared him to this classic, early production Range Rover. "The driving position is excellent, it feels great driving along and looking down on the world rather

Above left: The plate that tells the story... Manufactured by the Rover Co Ltd.
Above centre: Silver mascot won in a 'flapping event'.
Above right: At home in the yard.

than trying to peer over the tops of the hedgerows to see if anything is coming the other way. This is a vehicle that you can drive through a ploughed field when it's throwing down with rain and then turn up at a five-star hotel, as you're accepted anywhere providing you arrive in a Range Rover.

"As for its pulling power, I was at a show in a muddy field once and pulled three cars with trailers loaded with ponies out at one go, hitched together in a long line like elephants, trunk to tail. After selecting low ratio first and letting the engine just tick-over, the Range Rover pulled all three out at a slow crawling pace." **LRM**

classic LAND ROVER *monthly*

From trials competitor to Series One restorer,
the Lincolnshire magpie with a passion for...

ORIGINALITY

OTHER THAN a motorbike, and it's a long time since I last rode one of those, there is nothing like an open Land Rover for blowing away the cobwebs on the first sunny Sunday of spring. If that Land Rover is a near original early Series One, driven by an owner who lovingly restores the machines as well as being deeply interested in the history of the very first of the breed, so much the better. Pete Stringer is one of those guys.

I must confess that I have never owned a Series One Land Rover, but that does not mean I have no interest in them. Far from it. Indeed, when I first started my researches into the military Land Rover some twenty years ago, one of the first books I sourced from the library was Tony Hutchings' bible on the pre-production batch, Land-Rover, The Early Years. After all, if one is going to study a subject, it makes sense to start at the very beginning, and this treasure trove of a book does just that. Tony also founded a club for those interested in the early Land Rovers, known today as The Land-

by
Bob Morrison

Previous page: Pete Stringer's working 1949 Series One – other than safety features, everything is pretty much original.
Top left: Pete has tried to keep the engine bay on LKR as original as possible.
Above left: Rocker cover is a very early production type.
Top right: Hooking up LKR, (which works for its living) to a trailer carrying an 80-inch chassis awaiting cleaning.

Rover Register 1948-53, of which Pete Stringer is currently the Newsletter Editor, as well as handling registrations, being spares officer and running the Club shop. For relaxation, and to fund his hobby, he sells and repairs domestic appliances.

On being told that Pete is a self-confessed 80 inch anorak and rivet counter, one could be forgiven for assuming that he is a shy, retiring guy who is content to beaver away in solitude lining up the flats on wheel nuts on a lovingly polished museum piece. The reality is somewhat different. LKR, his restored 1949 Land Rover is probably 95 percent original, and only the purists would be able to spot the non-original bits, and he regularly uses her for fun driving and as well as to tow restoration chassis and body components around.

He also runs the legendary 'Grommet', a Nationals Winner Series One Class 1 ARC spec 80 inch wheelbase trialer which he constructed from a dead 86 inch some ten years ago. Pete uses a 1988 Hi-Cap as a working vehicle

and has a 1977 Series III 109 Ulster specification fire tender as his next major restoration project. His current trials steed is a V8 80 inch Class 9 Special, built two years ago, but which has not yet lifted any trophies, though he says that this is, "not the fault of the vehicle, more the nut that holds the wheel". It is meeting totally dedicated club members like Pete that makes writing about Land Rovers such a pleasure.

Today the Register has just over two hundred members spread around the globe, and it has widened its remit to cover all 80 inch vehicles and their owners. It was the first non-competitive Land Rover club to be affiliated to the Association of Rover Clubs, and participates fully in the wider club scene. Its membership list boasts some of the finest vehicle restorers and historians in the world, and their combined knowledge is second to none in Land Rover circles. Indeed even Land Rover consults them on historical matters, as well as requesting vehicles for time to time for static and dynamic displays. Club

Left: Bonnet hold-down clips and stand-off brackets, which rest against the windscreen surround when the bonnet is raised, are kept in original condition.

Below: With simple cab canopy fitted rather than a full-length one, I find the 80-inch at its most aesthetically pleasing.

members' Land Rovers are also regularly recruited as props and working vehicles for period films and television dramas.

Regarded by many in Land Rover circles as 'Keeper of the Grail', the primary aim of the Register is to track down as many early Land Rovers as possible and keep them in working order. However, over the last couple of years the Committee has also dedicated itself to unearthing rare original spare parts and to pursuing the remanufacture of unobtainable spares to allow its members to keep their half-century-old vehicles on the road.

Indeed, so successful has this policy been that the turnover of the club shop ▶

has risen several hundred percent. A quick glance at the list in the back of Full Grille, their quarterly newsletter, shows spares ranging from black painted bifurcated rivets at just 5p each through to brake fluid reservoir tanks at £33. If you need a pair of the special screws for bulkhead sidelights, you can even purchase these. Without clubs like this, Land Rover as a company would be unable to boast about just how many of its vehicles are still on the road today.

more in the pipeline

Although I had primarily visited Pete to see LKR, and hopefully be offered a spin in her, I also knew that he had one or two other very early bits and pieces in his collection. What I did not realise was that in addition to his current restoration project, the 95 percent

Clockwise from top left: Pete with current restoration project in his workshop; LKR instrument panel is virtually mint; a new fuel tank is the only major replacement, chassis number plate on bulkhead under bonnet.

original 149th production model, which has the rare silver chassis, he also has a pale green 1949 vehicle with body colour chassis and two bronze green vehicles dating from 1950 and 1951, awaiting restoration.

He also owns a basket case 1956 86 inch, though with a very original engine, which was bought just because it is the same age as he is. Then there is that Forward Control 109 fire engine, complete with working pumps and authentic wooden extending ladder. However, it was the Aladdin's Cave of body panels and mechanical components that really had me gobsmacked. The man is not an enthusiast – he's a magpie. If he lives to see the Land Rover centenary, I doubt he'll find time to restore everything in the collection as it stands today, yet he is constantly adding to it to

ensure that neither vehicles nor bits are lost for posterity.

Then there's his interest in tractors, but we won't go into that...

As we sat on the lawn, between LKR and Grommet, drinking coffee out of Land Rover mugs on a pleasantly warm mid-March Sunday afternoon, I asked Pete what had prompted his interest in the Series One. Having spent virtually his whole life in Lincolnshire, which is generally regarded as being flatter than a very flat place, there seemed to be no logical reason for his passion, though, he says, "we may not have hills, but we have lots of very deep holes". Fair enough.

first Land Rover

Some thirty years ago, while serving a full seven year apprenticeship in the motor trade as an

FULL GRILLE ISSUE 128

LAND ROVER

LAND ROVER REGISTER 1948-1953

auto electrician and engineer, he bought his first vehicle for just £42.

It was a 1950 headlamps-through-the-grille 80 inch, painted white and covered in flowers. Today, he wishes he still owned that very first motor, which at the time was little more than a means of getting to work.

It was only once he left the motor trade about fifteen years ago, to earn his living from domestic appliances, that he took up vehicle restoration as a hobby. Roughly a decade ago he became very interested in the early Land Rovers after building his first trials vehicle. Before this, he had joined the Series One club, and then the Land Rover Register.

About three years ago, Pete learned about the existence of LKR, which had been in barn storage on a Derbyshire farm for the best part of a decade. He

almost didn't bother going to see her as past experience had taught him that long term barn-stored Land Rovers tend to be pretty comprehensively rotten. Fortunately, he made the journey, and discovered that the barn was actually centrally heated as it housed the farmer's classic car collection, which included a beautiful AC Cobra.

The owner had rebuilt the Land Rover's engine and front axle, but had never been able to get it to run properly, so had given up. Canvas and hood sticks had been separately stored, and the only part missing was the radiator grille. After agreeing a price, Pete brought LKR back to his Lincolnshire workshop and fitted the correct distributor and carburettor, set the engine up properly, and found that she runs a treat.

After repairing a couple of holes in the chassis for the MOT, and

Clockwise from top left: Grommet the Trialer started life as an 86-inch; brass discs on recovered radiators give month and year of manufacture; Pete snaps up every restorable panel he can find.

replacing the leaking fuel tank, he had a road legal 80 inch once more. Since then, he has gradually refitted as many original parts as possible, with safety being the only thing allowed to compromise originality.

As the sun started to sink rapidly in the clear blue sky, it was time to leave Pete in his workshop, where chassis R860149 was awaiting his tender administrations. What had originally been planned as a two hour visit had extended into a full six hours, totally screwing up our plans for the day. But as we had been talking about, and playing with, what we both consider to be the most aesthetically pleasing of Land Rovers, it was a day well spent.

If you're interested in joining the Land Rover Register, check out *www.landrover-register1948-53.org.uk* **LRM**

KEEPING THE COSTS DOWN

A Series II Station Wagon transformed from beast to beauty, and on a shoestring budget

by
David Bowers

RUNNING A Land Rover, or any other vehicle for that matter, on a shoestring requires a great deal of improvisation, and I am sure that Bert Bond will agree wholeheartedly that his engineering skills were tested to the hilt with a succession of Series One and II models that included a rare 1959 Series II Station Wagon, which is the main topic of this article.

Bert acquired the Station Wagon in 1989 when it was in a very poor condition, so bad that he foresaw a few points on his licence if he had decided to drive it home to where he lives near Ormskirk. Bert recalled: "Although it was taxed and tested for the road, I wouldn't drive it as it was in such a state, so I asked the fella who sold it to drive it to my home, which was a sound decision,

Above: Bert Bond with his daughter, Ruth. Below: Bert's '59 Station Wagon – tested his skills to the limit.

as I later discovered the brakes were absolutely lethal, as was the steering, and the gearbox jumped out of gear at every opportunity.

"There were also problems due to a leak in the fuel tank and the rear differential had gone west due to lack of oil. A non-runner in real terms, but I knew that I'd find ways of getting it going again."

complete refit

After replacing the diff and changing the gearbox for a secondhand unit, Bert attended to the brakes next; a complete refit with new pipes, linings master and wheel cylinders. The last job was to bleed the brakes, a job that Bert had done on many previous occasions, but not on a long-wheelbase Series II. "This was very difficult to do and I suspect that Land Rover would have had problems even when these vehicles were brand new. I was later told that this was a problem with this particular model."

Bert then had to undo some of the

work on the brakes, as corrosion to the rear section of the chassis required extensive repairs. At one stage he considered fitting a full replacement chassis, however, after confirming that oil spillage from the engine had preserved the front section, he opted for a replacement half chassis on the rear and new outriggers – work that was carried out by K Motors of Preston, a firm that has retained Bert's custom for his Land Rovers over four decades.

Bert commented: "I've heard it said that they used the very best metal on the Series II, so these are not as vulnerable to rust as the earlier or the later models."

Sorting out the electrics came next, as the rubber insulation had perished beneath the fabric outer coating. Bert rewired the vehicle and he fitted Series III lights and dip switch. This was more convenient to operate than the original lights switch on the dashboard and the floor mounted dipswitch, which was so difficult to find in the dark and

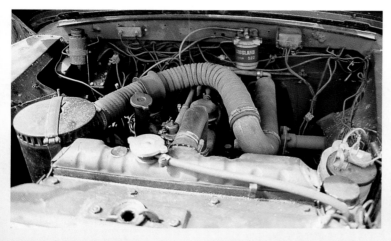

always required a tap dancing session before it was finally located.

petrol to diesel

Bert's Station Wagon arrived with a diesel, although the vehicle identification plate recorded that it had originally had an equivalent 2-litre petrol unit. That was in 1989 and this Series II was Bert's main form of transportation over the next 16 years and, other than overhauling the engine with new main and shell bearings, grinding in the valves and swapping the gearbox, he said that he has not had any serious problems despite racking up a considerable mileage over the years.

"The engine and the replacement gearbox have been fine; what really bothered me were niggling little problems, such as intermittent electrical faults, as for example, the headlights going out whenever I went over a bump. But I finally managed to get to grips with these in the end."

Fuel consumption was never a strong point with the diesel engine and such a heavy vehicle, so fitting a second-hand overdrive promised better results and this modification paid for itself in no time at all. "This came in very useful, and when you've had one, you could never go back to just a

Above: Diesel engine replaced petrol original; the interior has been meticulously renovated.

four-speed gearbox," said Bert.

"I generally use it as a fifth gear after getting up into fourth, although it also comes in handy when I'm towing my caravan or a large trailer, as you can then split the gears so that the power can be taken up in between two of the gearbox's standard ratios, and there's no loss of power that occurs when you have to apply the clutch. As for four-wheel drive, I've found this extremely useful when pulling my caravan out of muddy fields."

military traces

When Bert stripped away the paint in preparation for a new coat that was applied by brush and a steady hand, this revealed olive drab as the initial colour, which confirmed that this Series II had originally been used by the British Army, perhaps as a staff car.

Military use was also suggested by a couple of ▶

Above: TSY328 looks tidy now, but it wasn't always that way.

pieces of metal and the remains of a blind fitted to one of the skylight windows as a blackout, also holes in the front wings and the roof where radio aerials were probably mounted. Bert observed that a military-style electrical hook-up was mounted on the back panel to the left of the rear door, and the headlight bezels were painted rather than chromed, which he later swapped for civvy chrome items when a set came his way.

tale to tell

So much for the Series II Station Wagon, although Bert had a few more tales to relate concerning a number of other Series Land Rovers that he's owned.

"I've messed about with Land Rovers for many years and I often say that I've never really owned a 'proper' car. I started off with pre-war MG sports cars, a 1935 PA and a 1948 TC. The attraction of owning a Land Rover started to grow in the early sixties when I owned a supercharged MG PA and another MG enthusiast I knew persuaded me into sharing a Ford 8 as everyday transport.

"That arrangement came to an end when he told me that he'd driven onto a garage forecourt to buy some petrol, but then shot out onto the road again as the brakes failed completely. Enough was enough. What attracted me to the Land Rover was its separate chassis construction; I didn't want a rot box that could have folded in the middle. But I was short of cash, so I went looking for one that needed work in a local scrapyard."

Bert recalled that the scrapyard manager's tone and choice of words changed promptly from, "What do you want, lad?" to "Mister" when he asked if there were any Land Rovers in the yard that could be put back on the road.

"He said that there were a few Series One vehicles tucked away in a corner, but they were very rough, all beaten up and dented as if they had been worked to death in a quarry or on a farm by substituting for a tractor. I asked him if he'd got one that's a bit straighter and his response was: "What work are you going to put it to, mister?" I replied that I wanted one to use as an everyday car, but I'm sure he thought I was some kind of nutter, and that was that."

a regretful sale

Undeterred, Bert came across a more promising SWB Series One example on a garage forecourt in 1961, and even though the engine

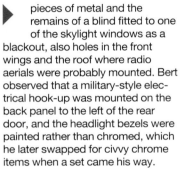

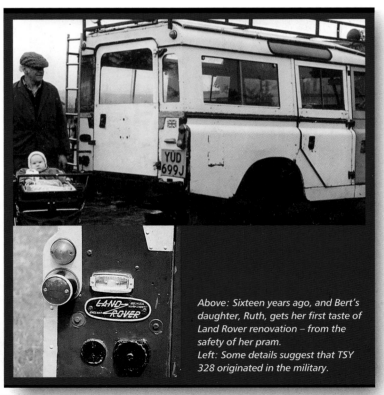

Above: Sixteen years ago, and Bert's daughter, Ruth, gets her first taste of Land Rover renovation – from the safety of her pram.
Left: Some details suggest that TSY 328 originated in the military.

Above: Ferodo brake efficiency indicator on the left with a Tapley gradient and trailer load weight indicator.

was so noisy, that it precluded all forms of communication but for hand signals, an exchange engine that came complete with all ancillaries barring a carburettor at only £78 soon resolved the problem. After fitting the carb from the original redundant motor, the Series One served Bert well over the years until 1972, and he regrets selling it to this very day.

Somewhat out of character after so many years of running a Series One on the cheap, Bert splashed out on a brand new 88 in 1971 that eventually replaced the Series One, although he says that he was in for a disappointment when it finally arrived after a long six-month wait.

"The salesman said that I was ever so lucky, as a new Series III SWB had been delivered rather than the older IIA model that I had been looking forward to seeing for the first time as its new owner. I wasn't impressed at all by the modern plastic dashboard that now sat in front of the steering wheel. I really preferred the old offset arrangement of the previous versions, and fitting a plastic radiator grille didn't seem like a good idea. But I suppose that I got used to it, as it is still my daily runabout."

Driving on a beach at Formby at weekends over the next ten years didn't do the Series III's chassis much good: although no doubt the owners of cars that had bogged down in the sands with a fast approaching tide were grateful for a rescue tow.

As the chassis was beyond patching, Bert than had to find another SWB for everyday use to replace the Series III while a new chassis was fitted. He eventually came across a likely candidate in the form of a 1965, IIA petrol SWB, particularly as he managed to beat the price down from £1,150 to only £800.

unforgivable intrusion
Returning to the Series III, Bert commented that he has managed to overcome his original misgivings concerning the dashboard and the unforgivable intrusion of plastic into Solihull-built products.

"I have to admit that the Series III does have some virtues, as for a start, unlike the Series One that was my first Land Rover, it does have a heater. I can remember driving single-handed and swapping which one was holding the steering wheel, as I had to stick one hand across my chest and under an armpit so it could thaw out: it was so cold driving along in a really bad winter with an icy wind rushing in through gaps in the Perspex windows. Those were the days." **LRM**

WHEN THE sun is shining, there can be nothing finer than an open-topped car, the burble of a V8, and no particular place to go. The UK has the highest percentage of convertible cars in the whole of Europe, ironic perhaps in light of the propensity for precipitation in this fair isle, but still we can't wait to strip down at the merest sniff of the sun.

As a working, or even day-to-day vehicle, a soft-top Land Rover is perhaps the least desirable derivative – with a distinct lack of successful weather proofing, vastly increased road noise and the associated lack of security a canvas top provides. But as a plaything, there really can be no equal and in combining the classic car appeal of the original Land Rover, with the mechanical underpinnings of a far more accomplished and capable machine, our feature vehicle this month will melt the hearts of any enthusiast of the marque.

Having owned a succession of Series Land Rover models since he was 18 years old, Mark Gray's ever increasing enthusiasm for off-road driving and greenlaning meant the hybrid route was inevitable: "It was

by
Jenny Morgan

Above: A classic hybrid – traditional looks with the modern underpinnings "combining the best attributes of the different models, in one personalised vehicle". Opposite: Chrome and brushed alloy detailing, and the most elaborate metallic paintwork ever applied to a Land Rover – the effect is visually stunning.

a natural progression really" he explains, "I wanted to combine what was technically a better (more advanced, capable) vehicle, with the classic look – ironing out the shortcomings in any one particular model by combining the best attributes of each into one person-alised vehicle. This way, you design your own specification."

The base vehicle was already a Range Rover chassis/Defender panelled hybrid and, although visu-ally aping a Ninety at the time, rather fortunately had a wheelbase of 86 inches and thus was an ideal candidate for a Series One body swap. Mark (with the help of asso-ciates at Tweed engineering in Dial Post, Sussex) stripped the vehicle back to a rolling chassis, and over-hauled the suspension, brakes, power steering and so on as a matter of course.

"The chassis work was clearly fine" he adds, "all we had to do was fit a new Ninety rear cross-member in the correct position for the Series One rear body tub." The donor Series One was more than sorry for itself. "For a moment I did consider restoring it but, other than the panel work, there wasn't much

worth saving" Mark sighed. However, all the panel work on this hybrid is from the original Series One, lovingly repaired and lavishly painted in the most stunning metallic paintwork I've ever seen on a Land Rover.

The colour changes through a spectrum between rusty bronze, orange, gold, pink to purple, depending on the light, often appearing as a completely different colour from one side of the vehicle to the other. "It's actually a (limited edition) Nissan Micra colour!" he reveals, "but the paint costs an astronomical £1000 a litre so not many body shops are prepared to work with it. I eventually found a company who specialise in Mercedes body repairs (Portslade Panelworks in Sussex) who were willing and able to apply it to the Land Rover panels.

body building
The bodywork is a combination of the Series One outer panels, a modified Series III bulkhead and a Ninety single piece windscreen grafted into place. Despite housing a honking great V8 under the diminutive bonnet, ▶

BEACH
BABE

When the sun comes out this funky Series
One hybrid just can't wait to get its kit off

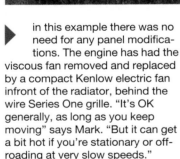

in this example there was no need for any panel modifications. The engine has had the viscous fan removed and replaced by a compact Kenlow electric fan infront of the radiator, behind the wire Series One grille. "It's OK generally, as long as you keep moving" says Mark. "But it can get a bit hot if you're stationary or off-roading at very slow speeds."

Mark wanted this to be a fun machine, a plaything, so in choosing a soft-top had a custom roll-cage built over the rear of the vehicle, which also doubles as a hood frame. The bolt-together pipework is padded with foam to protect rear seat occupants, and a custom made hood (with separate 'bikini' canopy over the cab area) was made by a local boat tonneau manufacturer to Mark's design which includes perspex side and rear windows. Despite a small gap above each door frame, Mark assured me the weather protection was actually very good, only at speed does driving rain enter under the lip above the windscreen.

Those of you familiar with the evolution of the Land Rover will know that the Series One was noticeably narrower than its

Top centre: General 'All Terrain' tread a good compromise tyre – better off-road than many due to open tread, but offers more predictable road manners than a full-blown MT.

Top right: Chrome rear crossmember very possibly a first on any Land Rover and typifies the thought, detailing and individuality that went into building this hybrid. Above left: Supple Range Rover springs offer masses of axle articulation – standard components have the effect of a significant suspension lift when supporting such a light body shell.

successors, and this is particularly apparent when the body is fitted to a Range Rover chassis and its corresponding axles. In this example, despite the addition of plastic wheelarch spats, the (admittedly huge) wheels are still a long way out from the body line. To remedy this somewhat, later Series and Defender vehicles have wider lower panels, with the characteristic rolled shoulder along the waistline of the vehicle, which can help to cover larger wheels and wider axles.

However, Mark wished to maintain the simpler Series One profile, so the Series Three bulkhead was narrowed slightly, while the Ninety screen is still as narrow as its predecessor above the waistline. Unfortunately, the Ninety screen tapers towards the top rail (whereas the Series One screen was straight), which meant the Series One door tops had to be

modified to lean inwards, following the line of the A-pillar.

Another modification was the inclusion of a Ninety fuel filler aperture in the rear off-side wing, together with a Range Rover locking cap. The fuel tank itself is rather on the small side having been reshaped to clear the rear radius arm mounting on the shortened RR chassis, and Mark is considering having a second tank made up to fit under the passenger seat to improve the range.

The underpinnings themselves are pretty much standard Range Rover fare – no tricky differentials or toughened drive shafts, but then it really isn't that sort of car despite looking like it can do the business. "Oh but it can!" Mark assures me, "but I've invested so much time (not to mention money) and work in this vehicle, I don't want to wreck it off-roading seriously. I know it can perform off-road if it has to – it's

got nothing to prove!" he smiles.

The engine is a standard carb-fed 3.5 litre Rover Vitesse derivative of the venerable Buick V8 – the Vitesse engine having slightly higher compression and a touch more performance than the corresponding Land Rover specification. Mark has replaced the airbox with a pair of trumpet style filters, and fitted improved ignition leads in an effort to smooth out any rough or weak spots in the engine's characteristics.

Mind you, it's the custom-made twin four-into-one exhaust system with a stubbly little cherry bomb silencer (if they can actually be referred to as a 'silencer') for each bank that really lets you know this is a V8. While some engines can sound like a tuned TVR, rather this hybrid has the far less subtle overtones of a Harley Davidson on full chat – marvellous stuff!

big boy

What immediately strikes you on approach is just how large this vehicle is when compared to our regular experience of a Series One. The bonnet is the height of a winch-challenge eventer's Ninety for example, the ground clearance massive with an 86 inch wheelbase and hugh 33x12.50 R15 General

Left: Range Rover axles vastly increases track width, while ground clearance suitably impressive on 33 inch tyres – although this hybrid rarely goes seriously off-road.
Below: Rear exiting twin tail pipes angled downwards in an effort to minimise the ingress of fumes when the rear canvas is open.

Grabber ATs. Although the suspension is standard Range Rover, the weight of the bodywork now is barely half that of the original donor, hence the effect of a significant suspension lift, with the body floating somewhere up there way above the axles.

"Mind you, I still had to modify the wheelarches a little to allow the 33s to fit" explains Mark – although this is more because the wheels are so far outboard, that on full lock/travel the fronts particularly turn in and touch the front edge of the wheelarches. The apertures were then trimmed with plastic spats in an effort to keep things tidy and the police happy." I could have fitted narrower tyres I suppose" says Mark, "but it just looks so right with this size combination." And I would have to agree.

polished and plated

Not only is the exterior visually stunning, with its ever-changing paintwork and chrome front bumper and rear crossmember (yep, he simply had standard Ninety items polished and plated before bolting them back on), chequerplate sill trims and the chrome 15 inch eight-spoke rims and huge General

tyres, but inside too is equally impressive.

The interior is fully lined in 5-bar chequerplate – the floor, rear loadbay, and door trims, together with the custom-made seatbox which is lower than usual to improve leg-room (thigh clearance) and locate the pair of sumptuous leather front seats from a Ford Scorpio, electrically adjustable and heated no less! Rather interestingly, the seats are now positioned offset to the centre of the vehicle (rather than the typical squished against the door feeling you get in a Defender) to allow greater fore/aft travel; and together with removing the bulkhead behind the front seats, the lowered seatbox means

Above: Standard Range Rover suspension offers far more travel and better ride than original Series leaf springs. 'Bikini' top over front seats helps to keep the sun off.
Below: The overall effect is a Series One on steroids – hybrid is huge in comparison to original example.

there is now a flat floor throughout the vehicle, with essentially walk-through access from the cab. The rear wheelarch boxes are topped with a pair of folding side-facing bench seats, offering seating for up to four passengers in the rear – goodness, it's almost an MPV.

The dash is the usual Ninety example, offering plenty of space, but nowhere to fix anything, but then in this vehicle there is no need for a barrage of switches, dials and toggles – this is a purist's machine. The V8 is connected to a Discovery five speed manual LT77 gearbox, groan. 'Groan' being the noise often emitted from either beneath the floor itself , or from between the drivers lips as the recalcitrant lever

hunts for home – Mark intends to change it for a four-speed auto in the near future.

it's in the detail

As you walk round the vehicle, you see just how much thought has gone into the detailing and finishing. The panel work, for what is essentially a 50 year old car, is exemplary – far smoother than even current production line offerings. The inclusion of original Series One rear lamps (found at an auto jumble, new, boxed) which have a built in number plate light; the micro indicator lenses so as to minimise the disruption to the classic lines; the subtle crease in each upper door panel that allows the frame to follow the screen profile properly; the

effort and expense of chrome plating the rear crossmember and front bumper – purely because no-one else has. The list is almost endless.

So many of us put our heart and soul (and the kids trust fund) into our hobby when it comes to Land Rovers, it's just infectious it seems. And Mark Gray's hybrid is a fantastic example of a passion gone wild. Other than financial constraints of course, with such a vast number of parts suppliers, product manu- factures and specialist engineers

out there, together with inspirations like this Series One, then I guess the only real limit is our imagination.

LRM

Mark Gray would like to offer special thanks to: Eastern Atlantic Helicopters Ltd. who are the sole UK distributors for MD and Enstrom Helicopters.

Tel: +44 (0) 1273 463336 or *www.easternatlantic.co.uk* for providing access to their facilities during ourphotshoot.

Above: 33x12.50R15 Generals are huge boots on any Land Rover. Series One arches modified to allow clearance on full travel.
Left: Chromed rear cross- member – 'new' rear lamps include number plate light.
Below: Series doors are easily removable.

TOUGHENED

A Range Rover that's had its tail chopped and its body-built for off-road life in the extreme

THERE CAN be no doubt at all what this vehicle is for – this Range Rover has been thoroughly reworked for extreme off-roading conditions, as the numerous battle scars along each flank will attest.

The original vehicle had already been chopped and 'truck-cabbed' by a previous owner when Jon Staff saw it sitting in the corner of a workshop. "I popped into AJS services to buy a windscreen wiper, and ended up taking this away," he smiles. In fact the friend he was with at the time actually bought it first, but decided to swap it with Jon for his Series III V8 hardtop (and the remains of a decrepit Range Rover), as he needed a more practical family vehicle.

The 1979 vehicle is essentially all the original parts, but had been retro-fitted with a 4.2 litre V8 Efi from an LSE Range Rover, and Jon has since replaced the previous Santana 5-speed manual gearbox with a four-speed automatic (with manual diff lock) which he managed to pick up for peanuts. "Friends told me to get it rebuilt, particularly as it was so cheap," he explains. "It seemed in such good

by
Jenny Morgan

Above: Supple suspension keeps all four wheels on the ground. Inset: Interior is tidy and clean, with seats from an Astra GTE.

condition I popped it straight in a couple of years ago, and it's worked fine ever since."

Originally built as a marshal's vehicle for hillrallies (he understands), over the past four years Jon has extensively modified the vehicle for a more arduous and active off-roading role. He is a regular visitor to Wales, and Northern France/Belgium with various off-road clubs and less formal groups, and the extent of the modifications reads like a wish list of aftermarket accessories and custom made fabrications.

Most notable perhaps is the full external roll cage, designed and built/fitted by Simion Hill at Bettaweld, specifically for this vehicle. "It's a one off," explains Jon. The cage follows the basic competition style, having a hoop around the screen and behind the cab area located to the chassis, with diagonal braces running back into the load bed. However, in addition there is a third hoop at the rear of the vehicle, with horizontal braces creating a square cage around the load area, and offering the potential to include a canvas tilt over the rear of the vehicle.

A custom snorkel is fitted to the nearside screen pillar, while the front and rear bumpers have been replaced by custom fabrications. Bryn Hemming is the man responsible for much of the off-road preparation on this vehicle, and Jon thoroughly recommends him. His inspiration is the North American Land Rover off-roading scene (as featured in LRM June-August 1999, and June 2001) where the vehicles feature elaborate suspension modifications, huge rubber, serious underbody protection and almost invariably monstrous V8 engines.

bumper to bumper

The front bumper is a very neat affair, constructed from square section steel, and incorporates Hi-Lift jack adapter holes at each end, a pair of ring eyelets (for recovery/winch rope return) in line with the chassis rails, and a roller fairlead for the Ramsey 8000lb electric winch located behind the radiator grille (which features a winch remote socket and kill switch key). Surprisingly, the radiator did not need to be moved backwards to accommodate the winch, but as there's no air-con. or oil cooler on

this vehicle, the available space was increased by removing the bonnet release mechanism and replacing it with a pair of quick release pins.

The rear end has had similar attention – the rear bumper replaced with a huge six inch diameter tube, shaped to fit around the rear quarter panels, and with a plate to locate a central combined ball and pin hitch. Above the hitch, and cut into the drop down tailgate, is the roller fairlead for the well-used rear mounted Superwinch X9. This is located on the rear loadbed floor (for easy access, particularly for observing the drum spooling when in use), bolted through to an additional cross member which is part of the roll cage installation, below the chequer-plate floor. When he bought it, the rear tailgate had also been drilled with a series of two-inch holes, although Jon is not sure why. Both winch cables feature safety hooks, which really are essential for the kind of winching this vehicle often undertakes.

As the rear end has been chopped by 11 inches, the original fuel tank had to be moved to it's new position under a fabricated (chequer-plate) cover in the rear loadbed, while the spare wheel is secured above. This does however quite significantly encroach on the available load space, and Jon intends to have a custom tank made in stainless steel to fit the void between what is left of the rear chassis rails. A pair of pivotable work lamps are incorporated into the rear corners of the cage, and the ubiquitous Hi-Lift jack is mounted across the top rail of the cage above the cab rear window.

clean and tidy
Moving inside, I was impressed how clean and tidy the interior was. "My friends call me a bit of a tart," laughs Jon, "but I like to keep the inside clean. After all, the whole point in having this vehicle (rather than a Defender) is because it is far more comfortable to be in, on a long journey especially."

Above: Vast amounts of wheel travel sees this 34 inch tyre literally hanging below the body line.
Above left: The rear tail-gate was drilled with two inch holes. Jon has no idea why.
Below: Rollcage with its additional third hoop and braces will take a canvas if required.

Suitable comfort enhancements include a pair of Astra GTE seats which have significant side support, and are fitted with Land Rover waterproof covers. The dash still has it's standard simplicity, with the addition of a combined oil temperature/pressure gauge, clock, a rev counter, volt meter, and more accurate water temperature gauge. Jon has also included a battery kill switch/key on the dash, which immediately cuts the power to everything. The centre cubby is a Range Rover item, with a padded velour armrest which as been modified to hinge backwards, and features an aluminium panel with the controls for the front ARB locker, the associated compressor, and a pair of in/out toggle switches for the two winches. Behind the passenger seat is an air-line and gauge connected to the ARB compressor on the seat bulkhead, and while Jon admits it is not particularly speedy, it can be ▶

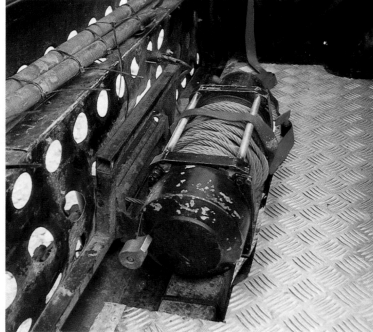

 used for re-inflating tyres after seriously soft off-road conditions.

Perhaps the most crucial 'comfort' enhancement is a rather sizeable stereo system, with a meaty Kenwood amplifier behind the drivers seat driving a pair of 16cm cones above the cubby box and a significant Alpine sub-woofer behind the drivers seat. The Clarion head-unit is in the usual dash slot (above the drivers right knee), while the rest of the equipment is built into a velour covered wooden box mounted against the seat bulkhead, and can be quickly removed if going wading for example.

US-style
As part of the truck-cab conversion, the roof and rear window surround was fabricated in aluminium, and the roof has been

Above left: 34 inch tyres on Mach 5 rims, vented and cross-drilled discs up front, lower spring cups extended by 1.5 inches and the steering drag link is sleeved.
Above right: Rear-mounted Superwinch X9.
Below: Rear end is chopped by 11 inches.

lined with a hard wearing tweedy-style cloth. A 40ch CB radio is mounted between where the sun visors would be, were those fitted, together with a roof mounted map flexi-light for the passenger/navigator. The internal door trims have also been replaced with aluminium sheet, with the original RR door furniture re-attached.

The US-style inspiration for this vehicle does not stop at the visual. Most impressive is the suspension and underbody modifications – this machine really has mighty ability. The suspension has been raised using plus two-inch springs all

round, together with extending the bottom spring cups a further inch and a half, and fitting plus two-inch Pro-comp Explorer ES3000 dampers. However, Jon intends to replace these dampers as the increased lift means these shocks bottom out before the vehicle runs out of travel. "The axles are hanging on the shocks at the moment – not a good thing," he admits. The front radius arms have also been bent to allow the differential to sit at a more natural level, although the front drive shaft is now at it's limit and Jon intends to replace this with a Discovery item which features a

double universal joint which should help smooth things out.

The front axle features an ARB air-locking differential, the rear has a Detroit locker automatic 'un-locking' differential (in that it usually stays locked, that is until you go round a corner for example). "It's a good combination," he explains, "the rear is fit and forget, and improved things enormously, while you have the option to engage the front locker as and when you require it." The front axle also has a bolt on diff guard, and the front disc brakes have been replaced with vented and cross-drilled items.

Jon reveals that it is possible to buy a kit that converts standard brake callipers to fit the thicker vented discs. "They're much better than standard, and with the sort of performance this vehicle has, it's very reassuring," he adds.

banana splits
Were the Banana Splits paint job and built-for-a-purpose looks not enough, what immediately grabs

you is the size of the tyres fitted to this Range Rover. Matt Lee Mach 5 rims in stealth black seat a set of substantial 34x10.50 (280/85R16) Simex 'Jungle Trekkers' which have a very open and aggressive tread pattern – almost like a cut bargrip. I imagined they would be horrendous on the road, particularly when wet, but Jon says they are surprisingly sure footed. Usually a tyre this diameter would be at least 12.50 inches wide, but the slightly narrower profile helps to cut through soft Welsh bog especially, and has the benefit of helping keep the tyres inboard of the body work and thus legal. However, their diameter means the tin snips were required around the wheelarches, and Jon has trimmed them to the profile of a Defender arch, and fitted cut-down spats front and rear.

Such formidable traction, together with 200bhp or so

Above: 4.2 litres of V8 power and formidable traction keep this Range Rover moving.
Below left: Many people build hybrid off-roaders by taking an ageing Range Rover and re-bodying using a selection of Defender or Series panels, but not this owner.
Below centre: Simex 'Jungle Trekker' tyres are surprisingly good on-road.
Below right: Wheelarches were cut away and cut-down Defender spats added.

pumping through the transmission means drive shaft breakages are not infrequent. Jon has consid-ered replacing them with the later 24 spline versions, but he feels the dramatic difference in cost (partic-ularly the aftermarket toughened shafts) would be even harder to swallow should he break one of those too. Therefore, he keeps a spare pair of drive shafts zip-tied to the inside lip of the tailgate, just in case.

In action, the cumulation of all this hard work and thoughtful design really comes to the fore, and progress over tight twisty terrain is effortless as to be almost dull. With plenty of power through an auto transmission, lockable front and rear differentials, and literally massive wheel travel at all four corners, this Range Rover is built to take on the worst of anything. **LRM**

WINTER SUN IN THE ATLAS

The Ninety proves to be an excellent expedition vehicle as the old *LRM* workhorse heads south to the Moroccan mountains

by
Andy Cutting

NORTH EUROPE is never a very pleasant place in January, so what better idea than to drive south and find some warm winter sun in Morocco? The original plan was to travel with a group of three Land Rovers and visit some of the more remote regions of the country. Unfortunately the others had to pull out leaving us to go it alone.

This would be only my second visit to Morocco, the first being with the comfort and excellent load carrying capacity of my ex-Camel Trophy 127 (**LRM** October 1999). It would also be my first long distance trip in a Ninety and probably the furthest that H20 LRM had ever been away from sunny Suffolk – the Ninety was owned by **LRM** for many years, but had never ventured outside Britain.

Despite popular misgivings about the cargo-carrying capacity of the Ninety for such trips, we easily packed everything we needed: fuel and water jerricans, food and camping equipment, tools and spares, and an additional spare wheel on the bonnet.

My co-driver, Richard Collins, had driven an overland truck across Africa some years ago stopping briefly in Morocco before continuing across the then open border with Algeria. A few years ago Richard went back to Morocco on holiday and spent three energetic weeks cycling across the Atlas. So we weren't exactly heading completely into the unknown and we were confident to face whatever the open road might throw at us.

Plans for winter sun were not looking good when we found that a layer of snow dusted France and most of Spain. We broke up the journey with a day off in Granada, where the locals obviously regarded the deep snow as quite a novelty and sporadic snowball fights broke out between adults on the historic city streets.

At least the Rock of Gibraltar was free from snow and, after a smooth crossing of the Straits by high-speed catamaran, the mountain road from Ceuta to Tanger was quite stunning in the morning sunshine. Things were looking up.

Driving in Morocco is relatively easy if you keep your wits about you – but even our combined experience was not of much help navigating through towns. Signposts are obviously not considered an important, or indeed a necessary part of street furniture and we found that the GPS and dead reckoning were favourite. We even inadvertently drove the wrong way down a one-way street but nobody batted an eyelid!

Top left: The famous 'Alhambra' palace in Granada. Above: Snow and orange trees in Granada. Below: The city of Granada covered in snow.

An almost deserted 'Péage' runs down much of the west coast to Casablanca, which is the best way of making good time to the south, and we comfortably made first camp at Sale just across the river from the capital Rabat. That evening we strolled down to the riverbank where, for a couple of Dhiram (6p), we took the short ferry ride across the muddy water to Rabat. It was quite charming, balanced in a small rowing boat filled only with local people enjoying an evening out. One of the advantages of travelling at this time of year was that we met virtually no other Europeans; it can be a big disappointment to hear an English accent after making such an effort to get away).

In Marrakech, largely by fluke of navigation, we found secure parking and a centrally located hotel. Plunging into the Souk (on foot) must be the ultimate test of your navigation skills and I defy anyone not to become completely disorientated. The Souk is a place that absorbs all senses;

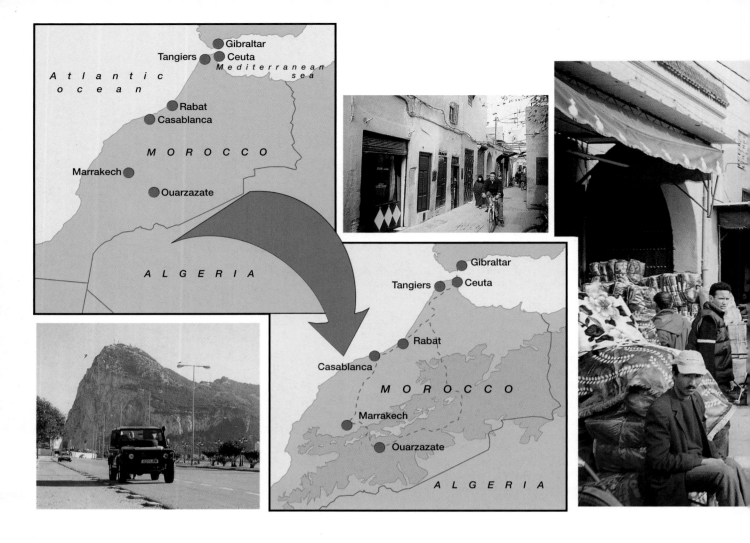

compelling fascination turns to panic, then back again, in the dimly lit labyrinth of stalls and slick salesmen where time has stood still for centuries. The place is so alive and the most interesting areas are those where the locals live and work.

Skirting the smart suburbs and orange groves bordering the north of the city, we sought the road to the Tizi-n-Tachet pass, our chosen route over the Atlas. Luckily for us the snow barriers were raised, but you really have to take your chances at this time of year. As we climbed higher, recently ploughed snow lined the roadside, not that it put off the numerous enthusiastic fossil sellers who leapt out at us. We stopped to take photos close to the summit where I left Richard to fend off two of these unfortunate guys who eagerly emerged from a freezing hut.

The road climbed higher and, after a knife-edge ridge with precipitous drops, a snowy rest stop marked the highest point of the pass at 2260 metres (7414 ft). It was very cold, but to be among these high altitude peaks was a truly awe inspiring experience.

back to the warmth
Descending from the mountains to the desert represented quite a contrast and was achieved in a

Above: Barber's shop in the Souk, Marrakech; Morocco and the trail we took.

matter of just a couple of hours. Ouarzazate is a desert town that also serves a number of film studios including the famous Kasbah Ait Benhaddou, most famously used for the recent Gladiator blockbuster.

At a restaurant in town we passed the time of day with a character who could have easily come straight out of one of the movies. From his facial features he was clearly from the deserts of the south and I struggled to follow his French as he described tales of illicit camel caravans crossing the Algerian border.

We followed the valley past Ait Benhaddou, driving on a very rough track for around forty miles winding up through Berber mountain villages. Surprisingly the valley is highly populated with terracing for agriculture and carefully managed irrigation, but how such a remote area can still support so many people is quite amazing. Each village has a school and, naturally, the children were pleased to see a European vehicle, although to see any vehicle must be quite an event as we only met two others all day. The children were well turned out with many of the younger ones looking like miniature adults in their long winter coats. As is the custom of the Berber people, everyone was

very polite and friendly always exchanging a greeting and especially grateful when we stopped to allow a laden donkey to pass.

Driving out of the valley at last, we walked up to check out an old ruin on a promontory. Out of sight below, the sounds of life drifted up from the valley floor: women laughing, the cockerels and the dogs, and the obligatory call to prayer from a distant mosque. Quite magical and we could have stayed there all day but for the cool mountain wind.

local produce
Unlike the tourist markets of Marrakech it is good to stop at local markets along the way, where you can walk about unmolested by salesmen. I had missed this opportunity on my previous visit and I loved it. You can buy fresh oranges or tangerines for a couple of Dhiram a kilo, fresh fruit and vegetables are plentiful – but we kept away from the butcher's stall.

You don't have to haggle to buy basic supplies, but a little gentle bargaining didn't come amiss when we each bought a tagine (traditional ceramic casserole) to take home. I was intrigued by the water carriers and buckets skillfully manufactured from old tyres and I kept a lookout for one made from a

BF Goodrich Trac Edge.

After so much driving we really wanted to spend more time out of the vehicle so one afternoon we simply headed out into the desert. Here the landscape is not the majestic sand dunes from the lids of date packets, but is strewn with small sun-baked rocks. We followed a wadi and just stopped for a few hours with the snow capped Atlas as a dramatic backdrop.

The absolute silence of the desert is quite overwhelming and at times it seems to be putting pressure on the eardrums. Even the slightest sound like a rustling paper or the wind catching a bush is greatly exaggerated. You can't help looking over your shoulder even though the chances are there is no other human contact for countless miles.

Above left: Narrow alley-ways in the Souk-Marrakech
Right: Foothills of the Atlas – lower part of Tizi-n-Tachet pass.
Above right: High Atlas–Tizi-n-Tachet pass.
Main picture:
Heading off into the desert keeping the Atlas mountains ahead.

Clearly this was no place for a breakdown and I was thankful that my considerable efforts with pre-expedition preventative mainte-nance at least lessened the odds. Having the chance to visit this kind of place really brings home why you choose to own a Land Rover.

cold for the time of year
At the town of Boumaine Dades we stayed at the ▶

excellent Hotel Soleil Bleu where we were the only guests. In common with most buildings, the hotel is of simple concrete construction and was absolutely freezing. However, the staff were very cheerful and friendly, in spite of suffering from the cold themselves (they explained that it was exceptional for this time of the year) and they prepared an excellent meal of lamb tagine and oranges.

At least daytime temperatures were quite comfortable until the heat started go from the sun at about three o'clock. We had a quick look up the Dades Gorge before deciding to take the Todra Gorge as our route back over the Atlas. Todra is firmly on the tourist route, and deserves to be as it is quite spectacular. The narrow gorge rises hundreds of feet above you and has a hotel built under a huge overhang.

Construction work was in progress to finish a concrete road, no doubt to give tourist buses easier access to the hotel, but this

Top left: Berber village on valley floor, one old ruin (Richard) leans against another.
Top right: Hairpin bends close to the summit of the Tizi-n-Tachet pass
Below: Berber village in the valley above Ait Benhaddou.

will spoil the character of the place. The road construction continues much further up the gorge and we engaged diff-lock as we carefully made our way past a massive grader working on the loose and narrow surface.

The gorge gives way to a vast high plain under snowy peaks, made even more spectacular by the early evening sun picking out the shadows on all the contours. Amazingly we were on one of the fastest and best surfaced roads in the whole country, but this came to an abrupt end at a village and we were soon in low range.

We were heading for the village of Imichil knowing that we wouldn't reach it by nightfall and would have to find somewhere to stop along the way. Snow covered the track, thankfully not frozen, as we climbed high on a perilous unsurfaced road without crash barriers.

Just before dark we came across two young Europeans with their Berber guide who, as it turned out, had been out hiking and taken longer than expected. In the already

sub-zero temperature we agreed to take them to the next village as there was little prospect of any other traffic. With all three safely squeezed in the back of the Ninety it was still a twenty minute drive to the nearest village where, under a full moon, our arrival caused quite a stir. Quickly we were ushered to the local auberge where the patron, Ottman, served tea and prepared a meal while we all huddled around the single propane heater.

devastatingly cold

At an altitude of around 2560 m (8400 ft) it was seriously cold that night and I mean seriously cold – I only wish I'd had a thermometer to prove it. The water in the bottle beside my bed froze solid – I was relieved that one of my last jobs before leaving home was to check the antifreeze in the Ninety. However, after emerging from multiple sleeping bags next morning, we could comfortably eat breakfast outside in the penetrating high altitude sun.

We had the chance to look

around the village in daylight when Ottman insisted on giving us the grand tour. We noticed the newly installed power lines but Ottman explained that the villagers could not afford to pay for electricity and the village water supply ran by a solar powered pump provided by a French charity – can you believe it?

In the winter there is little work in the fields for the men and, with the exception of the two blacksmiths shops fixing basic hand tools, most of them simply congregated around the centre of the village. Unemployment is a major problem throughout Morocco and we even met extremely well educated men unable to find any kind of work. In the village the women had looms set up at home and naturally they also attended to the daily household chores of washing rugs and carrying water from the village pumps.

We noticed that in most places, with perhaps the exception of the major cities, men and women don't socialise together in public. The vast majority of shopkeepers are men and you never see a woman driving; it's these kinds of thing that only really strike you when you get back to Europe.

We sat outside drinking mint tea until midday enjoying the peace and serenity of the mountain village during which time the only traffic was two old trucks. These old bonneted Bedfords are the lifeblood of these high altitude communities and ply the rough roads carrying supplies, people and livestock, often all at the same time. Referred to as Berber Taxis they are all the same uniform red and built to a design from the fifties, only now are they gradually being replaced by modern Mitsubishis.

It was great to sit outside in the sun, but with heavy hearts we knew that we had to get going. Ottman warned us that our chosen route beyond Imilchil would not be easy and he was right.

real off-roaders
Descending from the mountains the road all but disappeared and we found ourselves literally driving through the mud and snow and fording rivers – great stuff! But with construction work in progress it won't be very long until the tarmac snakes right up into the mountains. This will be a shame for those of us privileged enough to be able to make the journey by Land Rover, but for those who have no choice but to take the same route perched on top of an ancient old Bedford, then it will undoubtedly be progress.

The foothills of the Atlas really marked the end of our expedition, even though we still had four days of boring old tarmac to get home. We proved that the Ninety is quite acceptable for expedition use and that Morocco is readily accessible for even just a two-week holiday from the UK; it certainly seemed like much longer to us.

We had visited many new places and we met some interesting characters in an ever fascinating country. Next time there will still be plenty more to see and discover. **LRM**

Top left: Snow ploughed, high on the Tizi-n-Tachet pass.
Above: Todra Gorge with new concrete road nearing completition.
Below: Miles away from the nearest road.

HEAT AND DUST

Red sand and sweat across one of the world's harshest deserts in a 47 year old paddock basher

by
Ash Sweeting

WE REACHED the crest of yet another dune, surrounded by a sea of red sand. The 1955 86 inch then cruised over soft sand down the other side only to face another dune just up ahead. Freya, Rod and I had been crossing this seemingly endless desert for four days and hadn't seen another car since early the second morning. Despite the thousands of flies, intense heat and complete isolation it was awesome.

The Land Rover's journey to the Simpson started about ten years ago when we picked up the Series One for $500 (£170) as a paddock basher. Before long we managed to seize the clutch, after a deep creek crossing, and that was when the restoration began. After replacing the clutch, my brother Rod got a little carried away and went on to restore the engine, carburetor, radiator, exhaust, steering, brakes, shock absorbers, prop shafts, front differential, front swivel pins, fire wall and electrics. He then added a new set of tyres and got the vehicle registered. The body was deliberately left in the original battered condition to maintain the paddock basher feel of the car.

Sunset over the flat expansive Sturts Stony Desert.

On hearing that I was planning a trip across The Simpson, Rod jumped at the prospect of taking the Land Rover to the desert. While the vehicle at this stage was completely capable of negotiating the streets of Melbourne, and even the odd weekend in the bush, there was a lot of work that needed doing before it was ready to cross the only part of Australia that hasn't ever been settled by Europeans. The next few months were frantically spent preparing it and procuring all the spares and equipment we would need for the trip.

During this time Rod replaced all the springs and front wheel bearings and restored the front universal joints and steering rod ends. He also repaired some chassis rust, acquired some hood sticks and a soft top and gave the vehicle a thorough service. By then everything apart from the gearbox and the body had been restored.

water, water...

Being a short wheelbase we only had a limited amount of space, though it is surprising how much gear you can fit into such a little car. We had to determine what we really needed to take and what we could

leave behind. Obviously the first two items on our list were fuel and water. We'd decided we needed about 220 litres of fuel and 100 litres of water to get across the Simpson, from Birdsville to Oodnadatta via Dalhousie Springs, safely.

While Rod was preparing the vehicle prior to the trip he made an aluminum container that sat under the middle seat, suspended above the gearbox and transfer case. In this we put most of our spare parts. We also bolted a spare set of rear axles, which 86s are notorious for breaking, onto the bullbar and strapped a second spare tyre onto the back.

Somehow we managed to fit the three spanners that one needs for an 86, as well as a fairly comprehensive assortment of tools into the tool box under the passenger seat. Aside from these we had an air compressor, a set of tyre pliers and levers, snatch strap, towing strap and shackles in the back. The high lift jack was bolted onto the bullbar next to the spare axles and a regular spade was bolted onto the front guard.

With all of these items packed there was still loads of room in the back for an esky (ice chest/cool box) and a few boxes of food, cooking gear, three 'swags' and

three bags of clothes. All that was then left was our camera equipment, a GPS and the satellite phone, which we hired from the police in Birdsville and then returned it to the police station in Oodnadatta after we had crossed the desert.

After meeting Rod in the Snowy Mountains, one of the great stomping grounds for early model Land Rovers, we set off – three across the front seat. Flat out at 50 mph the 1000 mile drive up through western NSW and Southwestern Queensland on sealed roads was hot, noisy and slow.

As the sun was setting on the second day we finally hit the dirt and then continued into the setting sun, still at 50mph, to Cooper Creek and The Dig Tree. This is where the explorers, Burke and Wills set off on their journey to the Gulf and perished in drastic circumstances when their base camp team left only hours before

they returned from their four month journey.

After another night under the stars, this time getting attacked by thousands of mosquitoes, we set off soon after dawn to the isolated trading post of Innaminka further along Cooper Creek. We then continued another 250 miles along dusty corrugated roads through the gibber plains of Sturts Stony Desert to Birdsville, the start of our crossing.

By the time we reached Birdsville the Land Rover, our clothes and all our gear were ochre red from the dust that encircled us in the desert.

Hot, thirsty and tired we headed straight to the Birdsville Hotel for a couple of well-earned beers and a feed. The vehicle had not had any real problems and was handling the rough stony roads well. However a few of the suspension bolts needed to be tightened as they had come loose with all the vibrations.

The next morning we filled all our

Top: Sunrise at our camp just off the Oodnadatta Track near Maree. Inset above: Packing the car at Birdsville just before we headed out into the Simpson desert.

fuel and water containers and headed off into the desert.

soft and slow

On reaching Big Red, our first major hurdle, we lowered the tyre pressure to 25 psi and confidently raced up the dune. About halfway up the Land Rover sank into the soft sand and stopped. After another couple of unsuccessful attempts we lowered the tyre pressure to 20 psi, stuck the car in second gear low range and then steadily drove up and over the dune. This combination of low pressure and very low gearing was used to cross all the difficult dunes.

We were finally in the Simpson Desert, heading along the French Line towards Dalhousie Springs. Consisting of around 1200 parallel dunes up to 40m high, the Simpson is the largest ▶

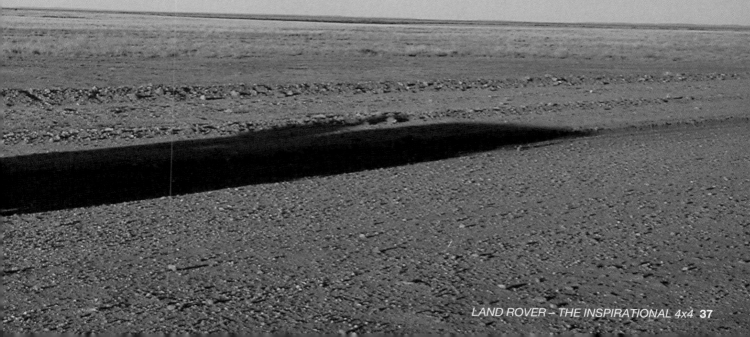

desert of its kind in the world. The prevailing westerly winds cause the eastern side of the dunes to be much steeper than the western side making the crossing from east to west the more challenging route.

We rarely travelled faster than 25 mph as we pushed our way along, up and over the narrow soft sandy track. At these slow speeds the transfer case stopped using oil. However, we still had to top up the water most mornings and the engine oil every other day. This

slow pace, combined with how hard the car was working climbing soft dunes, soon led to another problem.

The heat from the engine was causing fuel to vapourise in the fuel line, leading to dramatic loss of power when the engine was working hard climbing the steep dunes. This was especially a problem when we

Above left: Filling up with fuel at Birdsville.
Top right: Our camp just outside Birdsville.
Right: Sand dunes in the Simpson at sunset.
Above: Desert skies on the Oodnadatta Track.
Below: Camped just off the French Line in the Simpson.

required numerous attempts to cross the dunes. We have subsequently learned that this has always been a problem with Series One Land Rovers in the Simpson. Regular breaks in the 40 degree plus heat of the day to allow the engine to cool, combined with driving to allow maximum cooling between dunes, were the only methods we found to deal with this problem.

Just before crossing Lake Poepell, we passed the last vehicles we were to see in the Simpson. The next three days were spent enjoying the absolute peace and tranquility of the desert – wandering along the dunes in the late afternoon before being treated to some of the most amazing sunsets I have ever seen, then falling asleep under the stars with the only sound being the soft whistling of the wind.

hidden wildlife

The first thing I noticed after crawling out of my swag just after dawn on the second morning in the desert were a set of dingo prints a couple of metres from where I'd slept. They'd come along some

time while we were asleep to check us out and then disappeared back into the desert. While it's generally difficult to see it, it's amazing how much life there is in the desert. Many species of insects, birds, reptiles and marsupials live in, around and under the sparse trees, shrubs and grasses that litter the desert.

Apart from a couple of flat tyres and a small carburetor problem, we finally reached Purnie Bore and the edge of a seemingly endless desert. Here we reinflated the tyres and continued along hard clay capped roads to Dalhousie Spring.

After five days in the desert words cannot describe the pleasure of sinking into the 39 degree water with the golden sun sinking behind the horizon illuminating the natural spring with a warm orange glow. Then just floating there as the accumulated layers of dust and

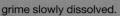

grime slowly dissolved.

Following a relaxing morning at Dalhousie involving numerous swims in the spring we continued on to Oodndatta in search of a timing light, as the Land Rover needed tuning, and a couple of cold beers, as the desert had left us pretty thirsty. While we didn't encounter any problems getting a cold drink at the pub, our efforts to find a timing light were unsuccessful. So after we replaced the points and the condenser and reset the dwell angle, we then had to resort to tuning the engine by ear.

A couple of hours in this small isolated town was as much of civilization as we desired so as soon as the Land Rover was ready we headed back out into the desert. After almost a week in the Simpson the Oodnadatta Track felt like a motorway. With the difficult part of

the trip behind us, we spent the next two days cruising down the Oodnadatta Track to Lyndhurst, with a brief detour to visit Lake Eyre. Then we turned left onto the Strezleki Track.

Surrounded by one of those amazing sunsets you only get in Central Australia and followed by a cloud of red dust, we came across one of the few creek crossings on the Strezleki. After slowing down and getting across the dry stony river bed I changed down into second to drive up the steep embankment on the other side. Then, as soon as I accelerated the engine started to scream, almost deafening us in the process. We'd lost the exhaust. Not too concerned, we pulled over in the middle of the road to check it out.

Over the past ten years the exhaust had come off the manifold

Above, clockwise from top left: Freya at the William Creek Roadhouse near Lake Eyre; how to fix a broken exhaust manifold with fencing wire; near Purnie Bore after we'd crossed the Simpson; Rod keeping our expedition mobile Below: Some things defy explanation really – the desert between Merty Merty on the Strezleki track and Camerons Corner.

a number of times and it was just an issue of waiting for it to cool before reattaching it and continuing on. But on opening the bonnet we immediately became aware that the problem was worse than expected. The manifold had cracked. At this stage we were over 200 km from Lyndurst, the nearest town, and the nearest cattle station, where we could possibly borrow a welder, was over 50km away.

Luckily we'd brought some fencing wire along and without too much difficulty or too many burns, we managed to wire the manifold back on. The engine noise was back to normal on restarting, so with our bush mechanics holding the expedition together we continued on.

The following day we left the Strezleki Track behind us and made our way through the Sturt National Park to Tibooburra and began our gradual re-entry into civilization. It was early the next morning that we suddenly left the dirt behind and were once again cruising along straight flat sealed roads. The Land Rover gradually clawed its way up to 50 mph and we prepared ourselves for the long hot trip back home. **LRM**

DESERT RANGER

The 'sand' setting in the new Range Rover Sport is sublime in the dunes of Morocco

by
Nick Dimbleby

IF EVER a car was made for the sort of driving conditions you experience in Morocco, then the Range Rover Sport is it. Tight, snow covered mountain passes in the Atlas Mountains give way to straight, smooth, newly tarmaced roads, all topped off with the impressive dunes in the Erg Chebbi that mark the beginning of the legendary Sahara desert. If we'd have had time to find some mud and a large piece of rock, we'd have collected the set on the Terrain Response dial in just a matter of hours.

Land Rover's off-road guru Roger Crathorne knows this well, and it's Mr Land Rover himself who's sitting in the driver's seat at the moment. Roger's spent months in Morocco at the wheel of various incarnations of the Range Rover: firstly in the late 1960s assessing the country's suitability for the launch of the original; again in 1991 for the launch of the Classic LSE with air suspension, and now in 2005, this time driving one of the most exciting vehicles ever to wear the Land Rover badge.

"Morocco really has got it all," he grins, as we whip along the arrow-straight blacktop in our convoy of

Top left: Purely for the camera's benefit, the supercharged Sport kicks up the sand.
Top right: Snow in the Atlas mountains and fast sweeping roads.
Above: Supercharged and normally aspirated Range Rover Sport take a breather on the dunes.
Inset: If you don't get stuck, you're not trying hard enough.

three Sports. "It's the perfect place to showcase the Sport's breadth of capability. We knew that in 1969 when Geof Miller and I came over to recce the country for the original launch, and just as the Range Rover has evolved, so has Morocco."

keep out of the way

Back in 1969, there were precious few tarmac roads, and those that did exist were narrow single lane affairs that operated under the chicken system of traffic management. In other words, if you're driving a big truck you rule the roost, and things would pull over to let you go past. At the bottom of the pecking order is the man on a donkey, and as a matter of survival, he's used to giving way to faster moving traffic.

Things haven't really changed much in the south of Morocco since 1969, but in the more industrialised north, dirt tracks have given way to high speed motorways that link the major conurbations of Tangiers, Casablanca and Fez. This being a Land Rover event, however, Roger and I are heading from Fez southwards in a big semicircle to our final destina-

tion of Marrakech. The Range Rover Sport may be superbly at home on the motorway, but we're here to stretch its legs as a Grand Tourer par excellence.

The Sport is, perhaps, one of the most eagerly awaited vehicles to come from Solihull. Since the gorgeous Range Stormer concept was previewed at the Detroit Autoshow in January last year, we've all been itching to see Land Rover's take on the sports tourer. First pictures didn't disappoint, but it's only now that we've been allowed to take our turn in the captain's chair.

And what a chair it is. In the Supercharged Sport that I'm sitting in, the driver and passenger seats are contoured to fit you snugly, while the interior is very much driver focused with all controls within easy reach. The sculpted high centre console offers a different driving experience from the 'sit up high' position we're used to in other Land Rovers. With the Sport, you sit very much 'in' the vehicle; but don't worry, chief designer Geof Upex and his team have ensured that the Sport has lost none of the excellent visibility that is very

much a Land Rover hallmark.

Our route takes us away from the airport, where the overcast sky quickly lives up to its promise and drenches us with rain, and hard rain at that. We've got around 420kms of sweeping tarmac to travel to reach tonight's destination: Xanaluca lodge just on the edge of the small set of dunes outside Maadid. Xanaluca is a favourite spot for dune hunters, and later we meet up with a posse of Spanish bikers on race-prepared KTMs practising for next year's Paris-Dakar.

In true Grand Touring fashion, the route takes us past many historic and well-known cities: Ifrane, Midelt and Errachidia, as well as through the magnificent Gorge du Ziz. Unfortunately though, we've got a tight deadline to keep, so we're unable to stop off and have a look around.

Accompanying us on the trip are six automotive journalists from Germany, along with Phil Jones, Koki Salvador and Moi Terralardona (three times Paris/Dakar competitor) from the Land Rover Experience and Joe Cusbier from Vehicle Operations. The four-strong support crew travel in an expedition-prepared Td5 Defender 110, which

brings up the rear with the sort of recovery gear you need for an expedition of this type and some spare wheels and tyres, just in case. Phil's keen to try out some new sand ladders that he's borrowed especially for the sand, and I reckon that it won't be long before they'll be called into play.

We arrive at Xanaluca just before sundown, and quickly unpack our things in order to have a look at the dunes before dark. Phil, Joe, Roger, Moi and I take a Supercharged and normally aspirated Sport, with the trusty Defender bringing up the rear. Playing to the camera, the Experience drivers have a go at the sand, but as we've a few road miles to do in the morning before reaching the large range of dunes at the Erg Chebbi, we elect not to lower the tyre pressures.

Big mistake. Within 15 minutes, both Sports are stuck in the dunes, so we have to walk back to the Defender (which is safely parked at the edge of the dunes) to get out the shovels and sand ladders. As the sun descends below the horizon, the five of us get on our hands an knees to dig out the stricken Sports, helped by a dozen local children who appear out of nowhere to lend a

Clockwise from top left: Can you imagine anything more fun ? Time to get the spade out again; Phil Jones from LR Experience lets the tyre pressures down; no problem going downhill.
Inset: Stretching the supercharged Sport's legs on a flat section.

hand. Many hands make light work, and with the price of assistance a couple of Extra Strong Mints, we're happy to have a bit of local help.

After much digging and judicious use of the sand ladders – which work brilliantly – both Sports are back on the move again, although one sand ladder is buried and is seemingly impossible to find. With the reward set at a packet of Cola Bottles, the local kids soon find it and we haul it out. By now it's dark and it's time to head back to the hotel for a well-earned beer and a traditional Moroccan supper of Lamb and cous cous.

range of dunes

With a trio of Range Rover Sports and a huge sandpit located just outside the hotel, it seems rude not to make the most of it; so at 5am we're back in the Sports again for another go in the sand and some more photography. This time we elect to let the tyres down a smidgeon, which makes the going much more effective.

There's no doubt that the Range Rover Sport is king of the sand. With just under 400 horsepower under the bonnet of the Supercharged Sport, there's ▶

prodigious power to take on the steepest dunes. Turning the Terrain Response dial to sand mode makes a number of adjustments to the engine tune, traction control systems, gearbox shift pattern and Dynamic Stability Control (DSC), optimising all of them to the unique requirements demanded by sand driving – power and traction.

As the sun rises, the dunes take on a magical quality, with stunning orange colours contrasting with deep black shadows. In the midst of it, the Range Rover Sports look absolutely stunning and perfectly at home; yet our senses are stirred still further when Phil and Moi power up a dune with the whir of the supercharger and the roar of the exhaust accompanying their performance. The Range Rover Sport is not a car that you can be unemotional about.

With the sound of the Supercharger at full cry still ringing in our ears, all too soon it's time to head back to the hotel for a quick breakfast, before heading out to seek the 'proper' dunes at Erg Chebbi.

In comparison to the sandpit outside Maadid, the Erg Chebbi are a serious range of dunes.

Above left: 20 inch wheels make great patterns.
Above right: The convoy comes to a halt in the Erg Chebbi.
Below: Phil, Moi and Roger get out the sand ladders and shovels to dig out a Supercharged. A quick push and it's out.

Although they only cover the tiniest proportion of Morocco's land mass, they're the sort of place that you could get lost in for days in the ever shifting sands. Fortunately, we've brought along our GPS, and – of course – the Sport's superb off-road navigation system means that we can input our waypoints and let the car direct us.

We enter the Erg from the south, driving northwards towards a radio beacon that is an excellent marker for the exit and our onward road route to Ourzazate. Unlike our play in the dunes this morning, this time we've really got to go somewhere, so there's little time for fun and risking getting stuck – instead we take the best route through.

For several hours our mini convoy tackles sand bowl after sand bowl, with seemingly only driver error allowing the Sports to become stuck from time to time. A bit of appropriate digging and use of the much-appreciated sand ladders soon gets us on our way, however. As the sun starts its descent towards the horizon the dunes get lower and more undulating, signaling the end of the section.

With only a few hours of precious daylight left, the convoy heads to the local fuel station at Erfoud to top up the tanks and reinflate the tyres. From now on, it's time to let the Sport stretch its legs once again and hit the tarmac.

on the road again
Despite the fact that I got up at five having only had four hours sleep, I don't feel tired – which is just as well really as I'm currently at the wheel. The Range Rover Sport is such a comfortable, yet engaging, vehicle that it demands to be driven, banishing any hint of tiredness. At the same time, however, driving the Sport is extremely relaxing – you get out at the end of a journey feeling refreshed, not abused. It's a strange paradox, but one that the Sport somehow manages.

Perhaps it's because the engineers at Land Rover have done a superb job with the chassis and suspension, offering a ride that is anything but jarring, while the handling (courtesy of the advanced Dynamic Response System) is amazingly positive on the twisty bits. Our route west takes us over the Jbel Sarhro mountains near Agdz, which – in true mountain pass fashion – features numerous switchbacks and hair-raising hair-

pins, yet the Sports feel planted to the road.

Switching the gearbox into 'Command Shift' mode (or manual, if you like), allowed us to enjoy maximum engine breaking and full acceleration out of the bends. Oh, and the Supercharged model also tunefully blips the throttle when changing down a gear, to seamlessly match the engine speed to the ratio selected. Marvellous.

For a vehicle that shares the much-praised T5 platform with the Discovery 3, it's amazing how different the two vehicles feel. I'm not sure if that's to do with the radically different cabin ambience, or the extra performance-orientated electronic trickery that the Sport sports.

Despite being assembled on the same line at Solihull, the two vehicles feel very different – which, again, is a tribute to the engineering and design teams that developed them side by side. With such teams responsible for Land Rover's ongoing product line-up, the continued success of the company looks very rosy indeed.

Today's route is just a small hop in comparison to the kilometres we've been driving the past couple of days, although as the route crosses the mighty Atlas mountains, the twisty mountain pass we drove yesterday serves as an appropriate warm up.

The snow-capped Atlas are our final hurdle before our ultimate destination of Marrakech. We're using the Col du Tichka on the main N9, which is one of the main routes across this impressive range of mountains. The road takes a tortuously long time to get to the summit, which reaches some 2,260 metres above sea level.

rock and roll

The final blast takes on more hairpins and other somewhat unexpected obstacles: local trinket merchants leaping into the middle of the road in front of us at speed, desperate to sell us their nuggets of topaz and quartz. There's only so much rock that we can take, so the majority of them pass as moving chicanes with the Dynamic Response system taking care of the roll.

There's evidence of recent snow, although the roads are clear, but stepping out of the climate-controlled luxury of the Sport's cabin at the summit brings a shock to the system – it's bloody cold out there; especially

Above left: Sunrise in the dunes is well worth getting up for...
...especially when you've got a Sport to play in, above right.
Below: And the beauty of driving in sand is that a few days later, all traces of our presence were erased. Tread lightly at its best.

when you compare it to the high temperatures we experienced in the dunes barely 24 hours ago. As we pass a sign in French and Arabic warning of icy roads, we acknowledge that this bit of road needs a lot of care to avoid any nasty surprises.

But, needless to say, aboard the Sports, we made it safely down to the bottom, where higher temperatures and the midday sun greet us in Marrakech. There's just enough time to head to the famous Soukh, buy the obligatory couple of carpets and then head to the airport for our respective flights home.

In the airport car park before saying our farewells, I ask Roger what he really thinks about the Sport – after all, it's a very different vehicle from the one he was driving with Geof Miller back in 1969, even though there's a strong trace of Classic DNA in the Sport. The man with over 40 years experience with Land Rover has an expression on his face that's like a child with a new toy. "It's brilliant," he says, with a grin from ear to ear and a glint in his eye. "After such a journey I feel great. I'm mega impressed!"

Well Roger, so am I, so am I. **LRM**

COMPUTER DOMINANCE

The most technically competent 4x4 ever built faces its toughest test so far – convincing the opinion formers that the concept really works

First Impressions
Richard Howell Thomas

IN 1989, Land Rover launched the Discovery into the family 4x4 market – a sector dominated at the time by the Japanese with affordable yet sophisticated four-wheel-drives like the Shogun and Fourtrak. It was a make-or-break vehicle for Lode Lane. Today, the Japanese stranglehold on the European 4x4 market has eased, but the Discovery is no less an important vehicle for Solihull than it was fifteen years ago.

On paper, the Discovery 3 raises the bar of technical ability into the stratosphere, but it's how all that technology helps or hinders everyday use that really matters. Which is why Land Rover have so keenly awaited reactions from press and dealers as they get behind the wheel for the first time.

First impressions count and the initial reactions from opinion formers often create a perception of a vehicle that lasts for many years into its life. Pre-launch publicity has already set the scene for Discovery 3 and we have all expected a vehicle of technical magnificence, dominated by computerised on-board systems – but will this be what Solihull's latest incarnation provides 'in the metal'?

Over the next six pages we look at the Discovery 3's unique features, styling and abilities based on real life hands-on experience.

LRM's editor behind the wheel as a Discovery 3 powers through sand – just one of the 'terrains' for which the vehicle has a 'Terrain Response' setting.

"Discovery 3 is the heartland of the brand – a Land Rover for the 21st Century – it is the next step in a massive transformation in our brand – exciting and very challenging for us"

**Matthew Taylor
Managing
Director,
Land Rover**

PHOTOS: NICK DIMBLEBY

RAISING STANDARDS

Purposeful yet refined, the driving experience is like no other Land Rover before it

FIRST IMPRESSION from the driving seat? A massive fascia and centre transmission tunnel cocoon the driver in a big seat and the dark plastic and fabric materials add to the sense of being enclosed in the cockpit. The Discovery 3 driving experience is nothing like the Range Rover with its bright and spacious cabin and 'floating on air' sensation.

Despite the fact that Discovery 3 is a big vehicle, it conveys a far greater sense of wanting to be driven than either its predecessor or the Range Rover itself. Everything about the driver's environment in this new car is purposeful – there are no fancy sweeping curves in the design; switches are placed geometrically; the instrument binnacle is minimalist; dials are clean and functional; ventilation vents are placed just where they should be; steering wheel is chunky and solid.

The layout is ultra modern and unfussy – it's been designed with a set square and a compass. Everything about the interior that confronts the driver is strong, determined and solid – the sensation is one of a vehicle that will get you there, wherever 'there' may be.

refined hush

Starting the TDV6 diesel engine is a revelation – or perhaps not, since it's so quiet that it's barely noticeable. A world away from the previous range of Land Rover developed diesel units.

As it also powers Jaguar cars, it's perhaps not surprising that this is a remarkably refined engine. In fact, it's so powerful and smooth that it really makes the more powerful, and naturally more thirsty, V8 petrol unit utterly redundant in Britain and Europe.

Lack of wind noise and vibration combined with the hush from the engine bay, translate into a quiet and relaxing ride. Land Rover have gone to huge lengths to 'improve the experience' for driver and passengers alike and the whole thing is a quantum leap from previous models.

The six speed automatic gearbox is all but undetectable in operation, so smoothly does it shift up and down the range. Unless, that is, the driver selects the sport mode allowing the box to hold on to the gears longer when engine revs make themselves more easily heard, or the manual mode when the engine's full output can be used to push this heavyweight along at an impressive pace.

Pace demands appropriate handling, of course, and this is where the Discovery 3 is so entirely different from the Series

Drawn from the Ford/Jaguar stable, the 4.4-litre V8 petrol unit (top) pushes out a massive 295bhp, while the 2.7-litre TDV6 creates 190bhp and a huge torque figure of 325 lbft at a very low 1,900rpm

II. In fact, it has to be said, that there's little point in making a comparison, Discovery 3 is a world apart from its predecessor.

The Series II Discovery relied on updated 1970s technology, derived from the original Range Rover concept – body panels assembled onto a chassis and solid axles supported on coil springs and held in place by various heavy duty rods and arms. It's the epitome of 'the

> *"Key object of the powertrain was to surprise and delight the customer"*
>
> **Steve Haywood**
> **Discovery 3**
> **Chief Programme Engineer**

Land Rover' and has served the company well for decades, but it's a system that has run its course and it has to make way for new thinking.

As it turns out, the all-round independent suspension system of the Discovery 3 not only gives far superior road performance, it also actually outperforms the old solid axle set-up off-road, too. The on-road ride is perhaps a little harder than I had expected – not at all the Range

The author drives Land Rover's UK managing director, Phil Popham on a test run. The smoothness of the V6 diesel engine means an exceptionally quiet ride inside. The additional body length of the Discovery 3 is clearly illustrated in this picture

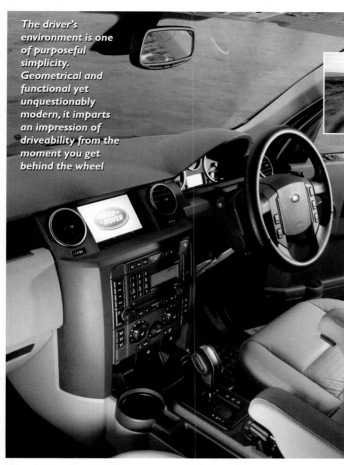

Rover's 'magic carpet' sensation – adding to the sense of the Discovery 3's driveability.

Rack and pinion steering, double wishbone suspension and anti-roll bars keep the new vehicle level and straight on tarmac. There is vastly more 'feel' from the road on cornering and body roll is comfortingly much reduced thanks in no small part to a considerably lowered centre of gravity.

Brakes are ABS, of course, and the handbrake is electronic requiring only the flick of a switch to engage – then it disengages automatically as you pull

off. Marvellous.

The driving sensation all this produces is one of being far more in control than in any other Land Rover vehicle. Discovery 3 is no sports car, but it's easy to drive and that takes much of the stress out of the whole experience – you don't have to

work that hard to keep it under control, doing the things you want it to do, when you want them done.

everything in its place

Elsewhere in the cabin everything is much as it should be. Front seats are excellently comfortable; storage bins are everywhere; so are drinks holders; independent air conditioning outlets ventilate each row of seats; the stereo (as I quaintly like to call it) is awesome; headroom is well, roomy; visibility is spot on for every passenger no matter where they sit; elbow room is wide, surprisingly so in the third row.

Nice touches include grab handles in the roof that gently return to their folded position rather than snapping back noisily; GPS navigation system that automatically displays local filling stations whenever the 'fuel low' light comes on; a dashboard display that shows which way the wheels are facing when low box is engaged; door mounted mirrors that automatically flip downwards when

"All the Land Rover 'design cues' – vertical and horizontal lines; command driving position; instantly recognisable silhouette"

Geoff Upex Design Director, Land Rover

reverse is engaged.

Overall, the impression is of driving a car that is uncannily 'capable'. It's a vehicle of many different systems which work together in many different situations to help the driver achieve the best performance at all times.

The diesel automatic is clearly going to be the vehicle of choice, and rightly so. Fuel economy in the mid-twenties, performance in line with most modern day family vehicles and a smooth comfortable ride – add to that outstanding off-road ability for those who need it and you have a vehicle that is quite astonishing in its ability to raise the standards of family 4x4s.

Richard Howell Thomas

All-round independent suspension, anti-roll bars, rack and pinion steering and a low centre of gravity all have a marked affect on handling. Body roll is minimal for a vehicle of this size

Over the page: Terrain Response in action

EXPERT
IN THE CAB

PHOTOS: RICHARD HOWELL THOMAS

THE RATIONALE behind Terrain Response, writes ANDY EGERTON, is to provide a system which selects the optimum settings for the various electronic controls systems at the flick of a switch. Land Rover identified 50 different types of off-road and on-road surfaces and analysed their characteristics. From this exercise they were able to determine just what the vehicle would require in terms of inputs from the driver to cope with that type of

terrain and the optimum settings for the vehicle.

Obviously offering a driver 50 choices was impractical, and defeated the objective of making the system simpler. So, by examining the characteristics needed for the vehicle to traverse these obstacles, the 50 have been distilled down into five main categories: general driving: grass/gravel/snow; mud and ruts; sand; and finally rock crawl.

Each is selected by the driver via a rotary switch located on the centre console, and each operates in an entirely different way.

"Discovery 3 can wade in 700mm of water and climb a 45° incline"

**Steve Haywood
Discovery 3
Chief
Programme
Engineer**

general driving

AS ITS name implies this is the setting for everyday on-road driving, and here the throttle travel is set short for a fast response and the engine mapping adjusts to give smooth power delivery. The automatic gearbox change up points will be adjusted accordingly and the air suspension is at 'normal' ride height and to give a supple ride. All the safety aids come into play, such as dynamic stability control (DSC), electronic brake force distribution (EBD) and the antilock braking system (ABS) are in their on-road mode and, as such, are tuned to cope with potentially high speeds.

sand

SAND DRIVING is the converse of all the programmes, with sand what is needed is power – and lots of it. Soft sand saps power and causes drag, eventually slowing the vehicle and bringing it to a halt. With the sand setting, Terrain Response alters the throttle map to give a more aggressive response, more power and a faster pickup. Likewise the auto box shift points alter, to late upshifts and early downshifts to keep the power at the wheels, while the level of preload on the centre differential adjusts to prevent slip and loss of power.

grass gravel snow

THESE THREE substances share one characteristic, they are all slippery and difficult to drive on. Too much throttle and the resulting power can see you spinning a wheel or, worse still, sliding off the road. In this setting, Terrain Response lengthens the throttle pedal travel to reduce the chances of driver-induced wheel spin. The gearbox will take the highest gear possible to again reduce slip. DSC will monitor steering inputs and sensors will establish if the vehicle is sliding and intervene as appropriate.

rock

THE OLD maxim is 'God forgives, rocks do not' – they are, in simple terms, a car breaker, and for myself some of the toughest off-roading I have done has been on rock. Here absolute control is a necessity and Terrain Response can help.

The Rock setting raises the air-suspension to its maximum, for added clearance and the centre differential will be at its most aggressive in response to slip. Hill Descent Control (HDC) will adjust, giving maximum retardation and the lowest possible ground speed for maximum control; the throttle setting will be set to the lightest possible. This will give a progressive response and prevent the vehicle lurching over the rocks and sustaining damage.

on-screen data

WITH THE vehicle data screen set to '4x4 Info', the display provides the driver with a host of useful information to aid cross country progress. In this picture the front wheels are turned to the right; the centre electronic differential lock is engaged, but the rear axle lock is disengaged.

The Terrain Response is set to Rock Crawling (Hill Descent Control has automatically engaged in this setting. Air suspension is in the raised (off-road) position.

The vertical position of each individual wheel is also indicated: Front left has dropped below the centre line while the opposite wheel on the front is pretty much in mid-position; at the rear, the left wheel is raised considerably while the wheel on the right has dropped.

mud and ruts

IF TERRAIN Response has a party trick then it is off-road where it has the potential to shine. Land Rover knows that the majority of Discovery owners are novices when it comes to the gloop. With Terrain Response, selecting this setting in low range will raise the air-suspension for maximum clearance, adjust the slip settings of the electronic centre differential to limit slip and adjust throttle response to a compromise setting where power is available, but over a slightly longer travel.

When Discovery is fitted with the electronic locking rear differential, the system will also control that.

For novices one of the most difficult things is determining the position of the front wheels in ruts, the on-screen display shows the driver the position of the wheels, as well as telling them other information such as if the differentials are locked.

Over the page: Star ratings

"Terrain Response will 'migrate' across the Land Rover range"

**Geoff Upex
Design Director,
Land Rover**

PHOTOS: RICHARD HOWELL THOMAS

THE VERDICT

the look - front

ONE SURPRISING aspect of the Discovery 3's design is how it changes its appearance from one angle to another. Flat on from the front it's tall and square; 'threequarter front' (above) gives a purposeful, impressive stance – the lack of a 'crease line' through the doors comes into play raising the apparent visual height (look at the profile picture on page 46, where the reflected light gives the appearance of a line through the doors and the vehicle immediately becomes elongated.

The overall impression is clearly 'Discovery' with a touch of Range Rover.

VERDICT: An impressive design full of impact.
STARS: ★★★★

practicality - people

WITH SEVEN forward facing seats that apparently allow 108 different configurations, the Discovery 3's practicality speaks for itself. Each of the rear seats can be folded partway or completely flat and each has its own three-point seat belt. The 'stadium' effect, in which each row of seats is set slightly higher than the ones in front, gives exceptional visibility.

It's difficult to imagine a more comprehensive seating solution for a vehicle of this kind. However, we're going to knock off one star because the third row of seats can only be lowered by stretching in through the back door – not very helpful if you're trying to load a week's groceries into the back in the pouring rain.

VERDICT: An excellent arrangement, far superior to the Series II Discovery.
STARS: ★★★★

practicality - loadspace

WITH EACH of the rear five seats in the totally flat position, the Discovery 3 becomes, to all intents and purposes, a van. In the same way that the 108 seat configurations make the vehicle an immensely practical people carrier, they make it a remarkable load carrier, too.

VERDICT: What more could you want?
STARS: ★★★★★

the look - rear

DISCOVERY 3's tail is distinctly different from its predecessor – most notably for the lack of a spare wheel mounted on the rear door. In fact, with Discovery 3 there isn't a rear door, but rather a split tailgate in the style of the Range Rover.

The upwards opening top and drop down bottom section are cleverly split asymmetrically allowing much easier access to the load bay where the lower tailgate is 'cut away'. The top tailgate provides weather protection too.

Clever stuff as the lines echo the previous Discovery, but the missing spare wheel takes some getting used to.

VERDICT: Full marks on practicality, but the jury's still out on the aesthetics.
STARS: ★★★

practical off-roading

"Terrain Response works continuously – not just in off-road situations"

Steve Haywood Discovery 3 Chief Programme Engineer

THE NEW Discovery 3 is unquestionably a spectacular off-road performer but, for the most part, everyday owners will have little need for its more extreme capabilities. So how will it meet the off-road requirements of the average owner?

The answer, of course, is totally. With a wading depth of 700mm (27.55ins), and all the tricks in the Terrain Response box, the average country-based owner is unlikely to encounter many situations in which the Discovery 3 will be found wanting

VERDICT: Everything an 'average' owner will need.
STARS: ★★★★★

the spare wheel

BY REMOVING the spare wheel from the rear tailgate, Land Rover's design team have been able to increase internal space without adding extra inches to the vehicle's overall length. Smart thinking, but it leaves the question of where to put the spare.

The solution has been to undersling it at the rear with a wind-down mechanism operated from the load area. How mucky the spare will get after a few months winter use remains to be seen, and should the wheel need to be accessed if the vehicle has a damaged tyre in deep ruts, mud or rocks, then problems could arise.

VERDICT: Not an ideal place, but it's difficult to know where else it could go.
STARS: ★★

the back row

USUALLY IT'S only the kids who want to travel in the third row of seats in a Discovery, but perhaps things will be different now. Two full size adults can comfortably sit in the third row and the picture above is exactly the view that a rear seat passenger will enjoy.

The 'stadium' effect really works and big people will have no problem on moderately long journeys. The rearmost seats have their own air-con on the top spec models, as well as hi-fi plug-ins and drinks holders – the kids will absolutely love it.

VERDICT: More thought has probably been put into the third row than any of the other seats and the result is brilliant.
STARS: ★★★★★

"There's space for a total of 17.5 litres of bottled drinks in Discovery 3's drinks holders"

Geoff Upex Design Director, Land Rover

does it all matter?

AND FINALLY... does the Discovery 3's box of off-road tricks really matter to the buyer who just wants a competent, practical 4x4 for everyday family use? The answer is yes, and no.

If all an owner will ever do is potter around town to the shops, school, office and cinema, then really any people carrier will do. But for anyone who lives a slightly more adventurous life – towing a trailer, boat or caravan, perhaps – or who likes to venture into the countryside, or who lives in a rural location, then the technological competence of the Discovery 3 will, at some point, have an impact. The vehicle's complex systems, working so cleverly together, will one day make the difference between getting there safely or not getting there at all – even if it's only snow on the motorway.

VERDICT: The Discovery's exceptional off-road abilities may not be called on very often, but it's comforting to know they're available if needed.
STARS: ★★★★

TAKING IT TO EXTREMES

**The Sport is no poor man's Range Rover – it's fast and exciting –
perhaps the most desirable car that Land Rover has ever made**

WE'RE FOLLOWING a small Peugeot hatchback along a virtually deserted country road in north east Spain at around 80kph. There's a double white line down the centre of the road and we wait patiently for the bends to unwind into a straight stretch.

The solid line turns to broken dashes... mirror, indicate, manoeuvre. Oh boy... It's my first experience of what a Supercharged Range Rover Sport can do – and it does it in bucketfuls.

Our heads snap back as the supercharger whines, the six-speed autobox drops a couple of cogs and the Sport roars past the Peugeot in rocket mode. "Oh yes," says a colleague from a back seat as we storm down the road and the Peugeot shrinks rapidly in the rear view mirror.

I like this car.

I like the way it looks, I like the quality of the build, I like the cabin environment, I like the handling, I like the comfort, I like the acceleration, I like the braking, I like the engine roar, I like the driving position, I like the super-smooth gear shifts, I like its adaptability.

Later in the day as it clambers rock strewn tracks deep into the

by
Richard
Howell-Thomas

Sharing the same 'T5' platform as the Discovery, the Range Rover Sport proves to be equally as capable in uncompromising off-road situations. The rock climb demo, above right, was truly awesome.

mountains, fords streams, fights deep sandy inclines and negotiates tight twisting forest tracks, I find that I like it off-road, too.

Built, as it is, on the same T5 integrated body frame chassis as the Discovery, the Sport shares the same attributes, but displays an entirely different character. The Discovery is eminently practical. The Sport is all about fun – this is a car that you would get into simply to go for a drive, just for the pure entertainment of the journey.

The Range Rover Sport's Brand Manager, Finbar McFall, reckons that the vehicle will attract a new type of customer to Land Rover – people who want to get noticed, he says, entrepreneurial types. He's not wrong.

If car buying really does reflect the statement a person wants to make about themselves, then the Sport says swift, purposeful and stylish. This is a vehicle for people who love life and who go for it – big time.

Sure, it's got a big boot, it'll seat five comfortably, the rear seats fold down to create a huge load area. Sure, it's practical in many ways.

But it's a car for people who don't have to justify the purchase. It's for those who want it, and they

want it now.

So, while it shares many fine qualities with the Discovery, it differs hugely and will attract an entirely different kind of buyer.

And with the Range Rover it shares a name and many of its looks. But it's as different as chalk from cheese.

Where the Range Rover is solid, impenetrable, dominant, the Sport is lithe, quick and flexible. The Range Rover is for people who have made it, the Sport is for those who are still getting there.

The Sport's Chief Programme Engineer Stuart Frith says they wanted to create a car that was "engaging and exciting". That they've achieved their ambition became abundantly clear over two days and 520 kms of hard driving in Spain.

With seats that are sculpted and shaped to grip and hold driver and passengers alike, and an ideal driving position with the finely adjustable steering wheel and snug cockpit with its high level centre console, the Sport is a driver's dream. Powering out of corners, braking hard on hairpins, cruising at any speed you like on the motorways, this is a car that makes driving

easy – the downside is that every journey has to come to an end.

While the Supercharged's performance is nothing short of phenomenal, the naturally aspirated V8 is no slouch. Driving it, though, isn't quite as effortless as the forced induction car.

Such is the power and torque of the supercharged engine that it mates perfectly with the 6-speed ZF box, there never seems any need to use the auto's 'Sport' mode or manual override. Press down with your right foot and the system picks the right gear instantly.

With the V8 engine, manually picking the ratios, particularly up mountain hairpins, is the best way to prevent up-changes at the wrong moment. Some people prefer to pick their own gears anyway, of course, and the ZF's simple push forward up-changes and pull back down-changes could hardly be more easy.

But spirited driving, combined with a 2.5 tonne weight, costs. The Supercharged's 'combined' consumption figure is quoted by Land Rover as 17.8mpg. The naturally aspirated model achieves a fractionally better 18.9mpg. The diesel version produces an environ-

mentally less daunting figure of 27.6mpg.

As has always been the way with Land Rover vehicles, off-road performance is class-leading. Everything that the Discovery 3 can do, the Sport can do, too.

Few, if any, owners will ever approach the limits of the Sport's cross country ability. The same Terrain Response programme as the Discovery 3 allows the driver to select the optimum system settings for the ground ahead – rocks, sand, mud, ruts, snow – you name it and the Sport will deal with it.

an eye for the terrain
Today's off-road driving skills require an ability to read ground conditions with a fair degree of accuracy. When does the grass and gravel change to mud and ruts? When would you use the cautious torque delivery and high sensitivity to wheel slip of the Rock Crawl setting?

Today's driver needs to know these things to get the best from the vehicle. The days of twiddling the red and yellow knobs are long gone.

The technology is awe-inspiring. Take the rock climb demonstration that the Land Rover Experience

Land Rover describe their new vehicle as a 'Sports Tourer' and driving it over long distances proved to be as comfortable and effortless as you could possibly wish for. The seats are superb and the fascia layout neat and easy to use.

team laid on – stopping and starting the Sport on a 60 metre long, 45° bare rock face, then turning at the top to inch down on Hill Descent Control, stopping, reversing, descending again at a quicker rate – incredible.

Or how about the wheel waving rock climb – one wheel after another first compressed deep into the wheelarches, then fully extended in mid air as the Sport crawls the rock bed. The system is fully worked here, engaging and releasing the electronically controlled centre, and rear axle differential locks.

Or the full power, roaring charge through deep, deep sand up a steep and twisting incline. The Sand setting means a more aggressive response to the throttle, upshifts held and downshifts coming in sooner.

That the Sport will do all that, then dawdle quietly through towns and villages before roaring off along the motorway at speeds of up to 140mph, is nothing short of astonishing. And after 520kms of hard driving the thing you remember most is just how comfortable and easy to be in this car really is.

Truly it's a vehicle of extremes. It's strong, it's effortless, it's beautiful. I love this car. **LRM**

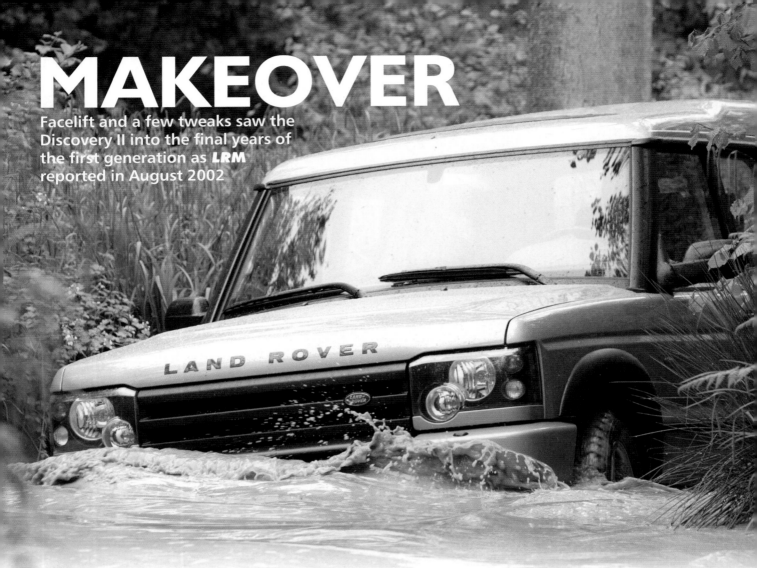

MAKEOVER

Facelift and a few tweaks saw the
Discovery II into the final years of
the first generation as *LRM*
reported in August 2002

WHEN IT comes to the sales
charts, the Discovery has always
been in the top three for Land
Rover and until the arrival of the
Freelander it was the company's
best selling model. With over a
half a million cars produced to
date and the Series II model still
selling relatively strongly, a tad
over 41,500 found buyers last
year, Land Rover know there is
still plenty of demand for the car.

So why mess with a good thing?
Well sales in the all-important
North American market have
begun to wane in the face of
younger more glamourous opposition, and in Europe the competition is getting awfully close in
many areas. With the all-new third
generation Discovery still a couple
of years away, Land Rover have
decided to give the current model
some tweaks to see it through.

So here's a new disco mix, not
so much Ibiza sound meets
garage as Discovery apes Range
Rover. Land Rover are claiming
over 700 part number changes for
the new model. The reality is that,
with new interior trim options and
colours making up a sizable chunk
of this figure, the real changes are,
in fact, limited.

Most noticeable change for the

by
Andy Egerton

*Above: No compromise
on off-road ability. Inset:
Td5 and V8 engines
remain the option in UK
and European markets.*

new model – should it be referred
to as a IIA now? – is the new
nose. Mimicking the style of the
new Range Rover, Discovery
gains twin round interlocking
headlamps with separate side
lights and turn indicators. With a
black background to the new
units, I for one think they look far
more attractive than the units on
the Range Rover.

A new grille, again finished in
black, now full width and incorporating thicker slats, ties in with a
revised front bumper. This new
unit again copies the Range Rover
look by having a squared off
design and incorporating the front
fog lamps. On the plus side this
new unit gives a slight improvement in approach angle off-road.

At the rear the indicator lights
move from the bumper up into the
body work and are enlarged, while
the reversing lights take their
place in the bumper. Also built
into the rear bumper are parking
distance sensors. Sadly the
bumper moulding remains
unchanged and consequently the
sensors look like the add ons that
they are.

A choice of new alloy wheel
options in either 16 or 18 inch
sizes become available. While

some of the designs are new,
several of the units were previously offered as options on the
outgoing Range Rover. A range of
roof bars are offered with a new
design incorporating thicker bars
to complement the new chunkier
look.

On the insider it's a case of as
you like it. The interior remains
unchanged save for a choice of
new colours, Land Rover Black,
Tundra Green and Alpaca Beige
and some tweaks in the audio
department. Having sampled vehicles with all three interior options,
all of them are pleasant places to
travel in, although the black was a
little overwhelming for my taste.
For a little relief from all that
blackness Land Rover are offering
silver trim highlight kits which
helps to lighten and distinguish
the interior.

Mechanically the new car and is
just as before, engine choice for
the UK and Europe remains the
2.5 litre Td5 diesel with manual or
four speed automatic transmission or the venerable Rover V8 in
4-litre form with a four speed auto
box only.

For North America Land Rover
will be offering the 4.6 litre V8
again with auto transmission. In

this application the engine produces 217 bhp and helps the new car complete the 0-60 dash some three and half seconds faster than the 4.0. Sadly Land Rover choose not to bring any of the 4.6s to the UK launch, so driving impressions on this, the most interesting derivative are going to have to wait.

On the road the '03 model Discovery benefits from some minor chassis modifications. Spring rates on those cars fitted with coils all round have been widened giving a smoother ride across a larger range of loads. This coupled with some adjustments to the front suspension settings and minor modifications to the steering give the '03 Discovery driver more feel and response.

Land Rover provided us with a test route from Solihull to Eastnor Castle, which took in a mixture of fast dual carriageways and twisty back lanes, giving us an ideal opportunity to test the new car. The V8 petrol ES specification came fully equipped as you would expect at that level. The new trim package, in this case Alpaca Beige, gave the car a light and airy cabin.

I have always enjoyed driving

Discoverys and the new car was no exception. Performance was as expected, but the revisions to the front suspension and steering gave the most surprise. Turn in and response was certainly better than other models I have driven, the steering feeling nicely weighted and far more precise. Some of that sloppiness around the straight ahead position that has you see-sawing slightly, has finally been engineered out and the car feels far more direct and placeable on the road as a result.

With the new steering set up, and active cornering enhancement (ACE), it was possible to hustle the new car along the lanes to Eastnor Castle with a degree of verve and still arrive without feeling shaken. Land Rover have also worked hard on the Discovery's refinement, new body mountings, noise reduction pads and revised seals all help to reduce sound intrusion into the cabin. Both V8 and Td5 versions showed worthwhile noise reductions.

So it goes well, sounds great, and now it stops even better. I have had the opportunity to drive Discoverys all over the world and in all kinds of terrain and never felt any cause

Top: Positioning of the rear lights has been revised. Above: New headlight looks so much better than on the new Range Rover. Above left: New interior colour schemes including this sombre black.

for concern with the braking department. The '03 model, however, comes with revised pads, a new master cylinder, new brake callipers and pistons. Add in some tweaks to the anti lock braking (ABS) – all models have ABS as standard – programme and the new set-up has more feel, shorter pedal travel. General use just feels far more secure.

Arriving at Eastnor Castle we had two very heavy downpours, the already wet Eastnor tracks, would be all the more testing. Heading out into the woods it was time to test the new Discovery's largest mechanical change – the return of the locking centre differential. This will a £260 option across the range and the difference it makes to the vehicle was immediately apparent as we reached the first slippery slope. The '03 Discovery retains hill descent control (HDC) and 4-wheel electronic traction control (ETC) but engaging the diff-lock alters the ETC mapping to take account of the guaranteed drive to each axle.

It works very well. A quick try of one of Eastnor's gentler slopes without the diff-lock had the ETC system chattering merrily away all the way up and we ▶

just made the crest. A repeat run with diff-lock engaged and we cruised up, ETC only coming in at the summit. Throughout the test the lack of ETC intervention was commented on by all. Likewise descents were made purely on engine braking, HDC never engaged regardless of the severity of the hills we traversed.

The test car was a Td5 manual left hand drive, and the new transfer box knob is now angled towards the driver, giving the impression that the diff-lock is engaged when, in fact, it's out. This situation is not helped by a rather small diff-lock warning light in the revised dashboard graphics.

Off-road the new Discovery is every bit as accomplished as its predecessors, the arrival of the locking centre differential has given the vehicle a new security off-road, if there is a gripe then it's the long travel throttle. It is still far too unresponsive for most advanced off-roader's taste, slow to react and indistinct in its power delivery, it is all too easy to stall the vehicle as a result.

The '03 Discovery has cost Land Rover £24 million to develop – a mere trifle by modern automotive standards – and personally I think it's been money well spent. The changes may not be huge, but the new vehicle is more refined and a more enjoyable vehicle to drive. Off-road the arrival of the locking centre differential puts the Discovery back to the top of the hill in this sector and gives it a crushing advantage over the opposition.

Even the new family face gets my vote, giving the Discovery a chunkier appearance. it may not have been big money spent, but it is a big improvement. **LRM**

Top: Eastnor Castle, Land Rover's traditional off-road test complex. Above and right: New lighting arrangements sees 'projector lamp' headlamps, rear indicators raised and reversing lights in the bumper alongside parking sensors. Bottom right: Fascia remains unchanged.

LOST IN FRANCE

Launching the latest Freelanders, Land Rover harnessed some French chic as Andy Egerton discovered in January 2001

by
Andy Egerton

NEW CAR development is a staggeringly expensive business. The industry average today runs out at around £450-£500 million to develop and tool up for a new product. Add in another £150 to £200 million for refurbishing the manufacturing plants, not to mention the fact that you tie up three to four years of your engineers time and you have the sort of figures most of us cannot even dream about, let alone comprehend.

So come launch time, it's vitally important that the new arrival is displayed in the very best possible light. The theory is that maximum press exposure will in turn lead to show room traffic and launch sales. To achieve this, companies will go to enormous lengths to show off their new arrival in the very best possible light.

Locations for the event will be examined minutely, companies can spend months if not years looking for a venue that meets their exacting requirements. Events are planned with precision; every aspect of the location, hotels, airports, even the weather will be checked out. But the most important single factor will be the roads. Every vehicle manufacturer tries to find roads that will flatter the various aspects of their new baby's personality.

Rough tracks through the vineyards are ideal for the Freelander.

So when I received an invitation from Land Rover to join them in France to sample the new Freelander Td4 and V6 I was intrigued. The rural back roads of France are not noted as being the smoothest nor are they the flattest, especially in the Beaujolais region where the event was to be staged. Would the new Freelanders really be demonstrated to the full, I wondered?

Regardless of the military planning and effort, this was an event that nearly didn't happen. Lyon, our host city, was at the forefront of the French fuel protests. The airport ran out of aviation spirit, the launch support teams en-route found themselves blockaded at the ports or on the autoroute and the advanced party in Lyon were marooned without fuel. With press coming from as far away as Australia, Land Rover faced the dilemma of possibly having to cancel the whole event.

With just hours to go before cancellation became inevitable, the situation in France began to ease and the decision to go ahead was made. A quirk of fate then saw the protests sneak through the Channel Tunnel and we Brits take up the fuel blockade. Yours truly found himself having to get to Birmingham Airport with a Defender which only had

enough diesel to get as far as the local Shell station let alone half way down the M6. A tip off revealed that a delivery would be made to the said Shell at four thirty in the morning, I joined the queue. Dedication to the **LRM** cause or what? Having had an adventure just to get to the airport, I arrived in Lyon to find that many other journalist's had not been so lucky.

With so many non-arrivals I found that I was in the unfortunate position of having no fellow hack to share the driving with, so Land Rover provided me with a navigator in the shape of Michael Rankan. Michael normally works for Vehicle Operations and, during the course of the event, would be a part of the team that will care for and prepare all the vehicles used for the demonstrations. A specialist body painter by trade, in addition to being press-ganged into navigating for me, he would be responsible for the repair of any Freelanders that suffered paint damage at the hands of the press. I promised him that I would do my best not to give him any extra work.

The misfortune in missing the event would at least allow me the opportunity to drive the whole route. The modern relief roads and auto route which bypass Lyon city centre

and carry much of the heavy north-south traffic would give me my first taste of the revisions to Freelander.

Our starting point was the airport railway station, a most curious structure designed by Santiago Calatrava. Built of sweeping concrete arches, and designed to mimic a huge bird lifting off into flight, we would, from here, head north out of Lyon and into the beautiful rural countryside and up into the verdant hills of this famous wine growing area. My first drive was in the new Td4 fitted with the five speed Steptronic transmission.

First impressions of Td4 were of its quietness; starting produced barely a murmur let alone any clatter at idle. All our vehicles were left-hand-drive French specification models which mechanically mirror their UK counterparts, but with some trim differences. Pulling out into the early afternoon traffic and filtering our way through the airport approaches was a doddle. The new engine is excellent, quick to respond and with a slick autobox, city and town driving was proving to be a snip with this combination.

Heading out onto the auto route it was time to see how quick the Freelander could work its way up to the limit. The answer was pretty damn quick. The engine is a derivative of the BMW M47 unit already

used in the Rover 75 and the 3 series, so it comes with a good pedigree. A four cylinder, sixteen valve unit, of 2-litre capacity, it has a unique specification for this Land Rover application. Equipped with common rail fuel injection, an intercooler and a variable nozzle turbocharger, the unit develops 112 Ps at 4000 rpm and 260 Nm of torque at 1750 rpm. This represents a power increase of 15 per cent and a torque increase of 24 percent when compared to the outgoing L-series unit that Freelander used.

I was impressed with the overall level of refinement - push the throttle hard and the vehicle is quick to respond. The gearbox would kick down readily and the engine always delivered its power smoothly and without sounding frenetic at any point. The new turbocharger certainly helps here, keeping the boost pressure up regardless of the revs and you never felt that that the engine was off boost at any point. Cruising was a relaxed affair, the noise levels never became obtrusive at any point; even when worked very hard the engine note would just become a muted growl.

The autoroute also provided time to take in other improvements to

Above: Backdrops don't come much grander that the Chateau de Pizay. Above: Land Rover's display bridge basks in the evening light.

Freelander, one of the first to strike me was the ride. I've always thought of Freelander as pretty good on road, well it's got even better. The chassis has received a number of tweaks to handle the extra power. Damper settings and spring rates have been revised as has the steering geometry. The end result is a tauter ride, firm but not uncomfortably so, it's well damped and does not float over long undulations as its predecessor did and coped with the ridges and occasional potholes of the rural roads with aplomb. Road noise was minimal and the suspension rarely transmitted any bangs or crashes back into the cabin.

The steering is also much improved, the power assistance gives just the right amount of help around town and for parking. On the open road it feels better weighted, more communicative at speed and provides the driver with enough information to know just how hard the front wheels are working. Coming off the motorway and onto a mixture of fast 'A' routes, dual carriageways and then working our way around some of the more rural back roads, Freelander ►

continued to please. It kept up with the traffic flow when required and Td4 proved to have plenty of power for the occasional overtaking manoeuvre.

On the back roads driving was a relaxed affair helped in no small part by the cabin. Freelander has always been a good place to travel. A light and airy cabin, good comfortable seats that provide plenty of support and an excellent driving position have all been carried over into the new model. Seat facings are now available in cloth or leather and the interior has also received some attention.

A new instrument pack, now fully electronic, has a revised layout which is clear and easy to read. Electric windows become available all round on the five door, while the in-car entertainment system receives a boost in the form of six speakers, additionally a CD player becomes available. Both Td4 and V6 also have the option of cruise control with steering wheel controls.

Best of all the heating and ventilation system, which was something of a weak area on the outgoing model, has received a total overhaul. Designed to cope with a wider temperature band, as has the entire vehicle, anything from minus 30 to plus 50, the system now has an increased air intake. This, coupled with a bigger fan, gives a minimum 15 percent increase in air flow across all settings. Air conditioning is also available; on GS and ES models it

Top: The Freelander in its many guises. Above: Impressive architecture at the Lyon Airport Railway Station.

comes as standard, and this is again of a new design.

A particularly hot and balmy afternoon in the south of France proved the capacity of the new units. No longer do you have to crank the fan up to maximum to get a decent output and the consequent reductions in noise are most welcome. On Td4 the thermal efficiency of the new engine is a little too good. This model will be fitted with a supplemental fuel burning heater unit as standard. This will aid cabin warm up and will be fitted to all temperate and cold climate market vehicles.

If there is an area where Freelander still lags a little behind then its the quality of the interior plastics. They still look a little cheap and thin, the new surrounding around the gear shift looks tacky and would flex under gentle finger pressure. The dashboard needs a little relief to break up the feeling of overwhelming beigeness. On the plus side the electric window switches have been relocated onto a new centre console which incorporates a small cubby box and oddments tray.

wine by the barrel
We pulled into the Chateau de Corcelles for a mid-afternoon break, time to reflect and refresh body and soul. Like so many of the chateaux in the area they produce their own vintage and the winery contained the largest barrels I have ever seen. The parallels between the UK and France are many, both are steeped in history and the Chateau carries the marks of more recent historical events. Its beautiful granite exterior has numerous bullet and shell marks that mark the last time France was invaded, the little Freelander sitting in the courtyard bears testament to just how much the world has changed since then. Built in Britain by an American owned company, with an engine made in Austria by a German owned group and driving through a Japanese assembled gearbox.

Leaving the Chateau it was time for the afternoon to become a lot more interesting, Land Rover had planned

for the route to take us up into the hills and there we would be able to experience Freelander off-road. The off-road tracks we would use were the access tracks up into the vineyards, rough tracks complete with outcrops of rock.

Leaving the gearbox in drive setting, it fairly romped up the first couple of tracks with traction control kicking in to help us over a drainage ditch or two. Nothing too dramatic, that was still to come, but testing enough to show Freelander's prowess.

Finding the next off-road section was to prove our downfall. As at most launches you're given a road book with directions, distance between way points and tulip

burning the clutch out.

'Interesting' would be how I'd describe the next couple of sections. Land Rover were at pains to convince us that Freelander has real off-road ability, the next section did. Tight and narrow, we had to negotiate a series of rock obstacles under the guidance of staff from the Driving Experience who acted as our guides. The low-down torque of the diesel and the ability of the automatic to creep, were ideal in this situation.

A particularly testing section had us negotiate a large rock step, the

sort of obstacle that would be interesting in a Defender 90 let alone a Freelander. In this kind of off-roading, control is everything and the auto is king. Lowering the Freelander down saw the nose drop as gravity took over and the tail was raised enough to lift a rear wheel a couple of feet into the air.

It was at this point that Michael decided to confess that he had not been off-road in a Freelander before. "I knew they were good but not this good." Which I think, is a telling comment.

The rest of the drive down was through a series of rough steep tracks. As before, Freelander is equipped with hill descent control (HDC), but for 2001 it too has been tweaked. It has always been a good system, however on Freelanders of old, when the system was engaged and you

diagrams for the main junctions.

With Michael reading the road book for me we had completed the route without any problems, but could we find the next way point? We weren't the only ones in trouble all around the valley were Freelander's looking for the same junction. We ventured up and down a variety of different tracks, minor roads and even ended up doing a little unofficial off-roading when we ran out of tarmac. We retraced our steps and tried again and again. We had done the thick end of 30kms looking for a marker that was 1.5kms from the last marker. Time to admit defeat, we were lost in France.

Like a border collie rounding up lost sheep the support crew

Freelander appeared over the hill to gather us all up and show us the route home. This took us once more up into the hills and into the high vineyards that cling so precariously to the hillsides. The tracks became tighter and narrower, these were neither well kept nor prepared, the Freelander however took it all in its stride. It's in situations like this that you have to drive the Freelander differently, plan ahead to keep out of the ruts although in places that wasn't an option and the vehicle would ground out. It's in situations like this that the auto has a considerable advantage. Keep a little power on, the wheels will spin and traction control will come to your aid. There's no danger of the vehicle stalling or of

Left: Beautiful Beaujolais country. Above: Some tracks caused the Freelander to lift a wheel way off the ground.

came over the crest of a hill, the electronics would take a moment or two to figure everything out and get to work. There would be a little surge of acceleration before HDC would bring everything under control. That initial surge and the fact that HDC would arrive with a bit of a jolt unnerved many owners.

For 2001 the system has been extensively reworked. Now reprogrammed, its operation is much smoother. The previous jerk and acceleration surge has been eliminated, most of the time you're not aware that it's in operation. On the auto, a switch behind the gear lever activates HDC; manuals retain the collar switch, and HDC will operate on first gear or reverse in normal drive mode, it becomes inoperable when the Steptronic mode is selected.

late again
By now we were running well behind schedule and we still had a 25kms drive to our overnight halt. With the support crew showing us the way it was time to try the new Steptronic transmission to the full. Produced by Jatco, this 5-speed unit will be standard on the V6 model and an option on the Td4.

It has been engineered for Freelander with a unique torque converter, gear ratios and a special final drive arrangement to allow operation of Freelander's four wheel drive system. It offers two drive modes, a normal automatic pattern gives you effortless cruising or for around town. If you want something a little more spirited then slide the gear selector into Steptronic mode. This switches the transmission into sport mode, allowing the engine to hold higher revs for better acceleration and earlier down changes for a better response.

Operation is simplicity itself, tap the gear forward for an upshift and back for a down change. In practice it works very well allowing you to hold the gear and accelerate with a degree of gusto. Downshifts for, say,

Above: The track crumbled stranding the Freelander. Some muscle shifted it, but by then the clutch was cooked.

a hairpin bend are quickly and easily accomplished, the electronics will match engine to road speed giving a smooth shift, and allowing you to power out.

the essence of France
Chateau de Pizay, a beautiful 14th Century castle was our overnight halt. Set in its own grounds with formal gardens and, naturally, its own winery, it was the quintessential essence of France. As this was my first visit to France, I was beginning to appreciate why so many members of my family are so attracted to the country.

The day dawned clear and cool, the first tints of autumn reflected in the Freelanders' paintwork as they basked in the early morning sun that peaked from behind the Chateau's tree-lined drive. The soft light and morning mist gave the area a feeling of tranquillity, it was almost a pity to have to get the Freelanders dirty, but hey, time for some fun.

Once again I was without a navigator, so Donna Flint from the press office volunteered to read the road book for me. The format was to be broadly similar to before, follow the road book from the chateau back to the airport. However, as we left, we were unaware just how reliant we would be on Donna's map reading skills.

Today's Freelander was a top of the line V6 three door hardback, complete with leather interior. This was the first opportunity I'd had to try the V6, the engine is a derivative of the Rover unit used in the 75. Here in Freelander, the quad cam 2.5litre unit develops power of 177Ps and torque of 240Nm which is roughly a 50 percent increase over the existing 1.8 petrol unit.

On the road the difference is immediately apparent, at last we have a petrol Freelander with decent performance. Acceleration in the lower gears is excellent, with plenty of power at the lower end of the rev band to enable you get off the line with some alacrity.

The first couple of road sections passed without incident, the V6 is proving to be a fine travelling companion, the engine's torque is proving ample as we wind our way around the rural back roads. It does, however, start to get its second wind as the revs rise above 3000. With a transmission system that predominately favours the front wheels, there is a degree of torque steer if you floor the throttle very hard. The cabin of the three-door is virtually the same as the five, although I did find that visibility was a little more

restricted in the three door at angled junctions and when reversing.

Heading off-road and today's tracks were similar to those we had covered in the Td4. Running up through the vineyards the V6 was proving to be just as capable. We tried a couple of climbs with just a trace of throttle and there was sufficient torque to pull us through. On a couple of descents I tried coming down without using HDC, there is noticeably less engine braking than the same experiment with the Td4.

This coupled with the extra weight of the V6 up front adds up to a little more momentum than most owners will feel comfortable with on a descent. Engaging HDC, though, brings everything back under control.

As we came to the next off-road section we caught up with another Freelander. In accordance with the best off-roading etiquette we allowed them a little space and watched them begin the climb up along a track. The route was bordered by a stone wall and a drainage ditch on the right and drop into the vineyard on the left. The Freelander continued to climb and we began to follow behind, a sudden lurch to the right from the vehicle in front alerted us to the fact that all was not well, Donna and I watched and held our breath.

Part of the side of the track had given way and deflected the Freelander into the ditch, which it turned out was deceptively deep. The vehicle was being driven by Land Rover's Director of Design, Geoff Upex and with him was Nicola

Forwards it would have to be, but the depth of the ditch was proving to be troublesome. We packed the front wheel with as many rocks as we could find and gave it a go. The Freelander refused to climb out. A second attempt with more packing and all of us pushing was a little more successful, but we still couldn't coax the Freelander back on to the track. The soft sides of the ditch were just breaking up, giving almost no traction.

We decided on one last go, the

Top: The Freelander is, of course, essentially a road vehicle and in its new V6 and Td4 configuration, it performs that role with greatly enhanced performance

vehicle was going no further until the clutch had cooled. I was pretty damned impressed that it came out at all. A damage inspection revealed a few scratches and a damaged door mirror.

There was nothing to do but kick our heels and wait for the clutch to cool and chat about Land Rover's future, my lack of enthusiasm for Freelander (sorry Geoff), France and life in general. It was a pleasant location, the sun was warm and the company inter-

Burdett from BBC RadioWM. Not the best kind of publicity, but a situation that had been totally unavoidable.

The next problem would be getting Geoff out. There was insufficient clearance to get my vehicle around Geoff's and even if I could we had no rope for a tow. No, it was going to have to come out under its own power or we would have to wait to be rescued. The vehicle was a manual Td4 and Geoff tried to reverse out, only to find the rear would ground out and lift the back wheels.

clutch was beginning to smell and there was the danger that the vehicle could simply slide further into the ditch. Geoff really went for it on this occasion, he had no alternative other than to slip the clutch to get enough power to the wheels and to let the traction control system be effective. The tyres finally found some grip and with a cheer from us all, out popped the Freelander.

But there had been a price to pay, the sweet smell of the vineyards was replaced with the overwhelming acrid smell of overheated clutch. We had got the Freelander out but that

esting, I can think of worse ways to kill half an hour. But time was beginning to press, we had to be at Lyon airport by midday for our flight back to Blighty.

The Td4 still had no drive and the best option was to roll it down to the farm at the bottom of the hill and continue in the V6. With Nicola and Geoff aboard plus their luggage, the V6 was destined to be tested in a way that Land Rover never intended.

With roughly two thirds of the road book still to complete and the amount of ▶

time lost, we knew we were going to have difficulty in getting to the airport on time. We elected to follow the road book until we hit a main route and then head directly to the airport. Another off-road section proved that even four-up the Freelander is quite capable, it would ground out perhaps a little more with the extra weight at the rear and I needed traction control to help on a couple of occasions but we made it through.

As we came off the last section fate would deal us a kind hand. We met one of the support trucks and fortunately they had one of the ubiquitous Michelin maps for the area and were able to show us our exact location.

Below: With care and a little expert guidance, a Freelander will tackle some surprisingly tricky terrain.

better and the ride was smooth. Turning into fast bends proved just how competent Freelander's road holding is, there is a degree of body roll, but nothing too dramatic. The chassis has plenty of grip and in normal driving the vehicle is a neutral handler. Push a little too hard and it will develop a degree of understeer.

Ancient tractors with grossly overladen trailers would lumber out of the fields on their way to the winery without a care in the world let alone regard for other road users. Fortunately the brakes have been upgraded across the range for the new models. Bigger vented front discs and larger rear drums come with electronic brake distribution and ABS. They feel sharp,

tunity is taken and it feels capable and sure, there was ample power for every manoeuvre. We finally hit the auto route and it was time to try the V6's cruising capabilities.

Knocking the Steptronic back into normal mode for more relaxed cruising, I found that the gearbox had a tendency to kick down when we encountered a long climb.

Nicola enquires just how fast we a going. "Quick enough for a thousand Franc fine," I reply. The speedo is nudging 165kph and yet the Freelander is still pulling well. The noise levels do become a little wearing at this speed, but we have no option other than to continue. As we start to hit the heavy traffic on the city's ring road, an amalgam of motorways, tunnels and busy

It was worse than we thought. It was at least 24kms to the main route, then roughly 80 to Lyon and we would have to negotiate the ring road around the city to the airport. Our arrival would depend on Donna's map reading, my driving and the prowess of the Freelander. We had no choice other than to go for it.

I had to drive as quickly as I could on that first section, the road hugged the valley sides as it wound its way down to the RN6. With the V6 set in Steptronic mode it proved ideal for tackling the fast valley road, change down for the hairpins and then power out. With four-up the ride felt more compliant - the springs were definitely working

strong and with plenty of pedal feel.

We finally made the RN6, a fast single carriageway road and hoped to make up a little time. Progress is painfully difficult, slow lorries, tractors and the general pace of rural French life do their best to delay us. The Freelander though is up to the challenge, every overtaking oppor-

intersections our nerves are tense, the signs say its still 12kms to the airport. A quick blast up the toll motorway and we can see the airport - there is a palpable sigh of relief from us all. Land Rover have a chap waiting to collect the vehicle from us and we make the check in with just minutes to spare. **LRM**

---

on reflection

ON THE flight home it was time to reflect. I've never really liked Freelander, a fact that has had several people at Land Rover taking me to task on occasions. I've always thought of it as more of a car than a Land Rover. But in France I drove one harder, faster, over more testing terrain and in ways I never had before.

We threw the road book out of the window

and with it went my preconceptions. Freelander is not dissimilar to that other famous product of the region we've just visited, the Beaujolais Nouveau. Lots of people bought Freelander when it first arrived and they got a reasonable product. Three years on and Freelander has, like a fine wine, matured. It's now a more complete package.

It can wear its green oval with pride.

LAND ROVER monthly

SPANNING THE YEARS
LAND ROVERS FROM COVER TO COVER

ON SALE EVERY MONTH AT WHSMITH
AND ALL GOOD NEWSAGENTS

HOW DOES IT MAKE YOU FEEL?

by
Richard Howell Thomas

ASK A dozen people what they think of the new Range Rover and you'll probably get a dozen different views. The contributors to this magazine are typical of that. All fans of Land Rover products, their opinions on most things differ widely, but especially so on this latest vehicle from Solihull. One thinks its looks

Above: Ground clearance is surprisingly impressive. The air suspension works independently on each wheel to give huge wheel articulation. Below: Keep the power on and let the systems do the work.

are fabulous, another doesn't like its appearance at all. One thinks it's good value for money considering the amount of technology on board, another won't spend that amount in a lifetime of buying vehicles. One cannot believe that any vehicle without beam axles is really a Land Rover, another finds the manufacturer's lateral thinking in the suspension department inspiring.

The brutal truth is, of course, that none of these opinions really matter. Not one of us will be trotting down to our local dealership to trade in a second generation Range Rover for one of these new machines. What really matters is how the well-heeled regulars in the franchised showrooms react.

Along with the rest of the specialist 4x4 press, **LRM** was allowed a day's driving on Land Rover's test facilities at Gaydon. But how do you 'test' a vehicle like this in a single day?

Testing its off-road abilities in the extreme is pointless – new owners will have only a passing interest in the vehicle's abilities in this regard. Will it be great off-road? Good heavens, of course it will, it's been developed and created by the finest 4x4 vehicle technicians in the world.

Testing its on-road manners is also something of a formality. At the price this thing's going to cost it would be an absolute disgrace if it didn't handle superbly. Likewise comparing it to older models is nothing more than a diversion.

What's really important is how does it make you feel?

You could take a degree in car purchasing decisions but, with a vehicle in this class, it all boils down to the image business. How does it make me look?

The Range Rover was never really intended as a status definer when it was conceived in the late sixties, but it soon became one. It took to its role with a passion, of course, and has dominated the gravel drives of the rural wealthy ever since. But where the second generation Range Rover was a little shame-faced about having

Packed with just about every
motoring gizmo known to humanity, the
new Range Rover can look after itself come what may

ousted the Classic, the new model has no problem with that concept at all.

This new Range Rover is the Sumo wrestler of 4x4s. It's huge, it's immensely strong, it's built like a hippopotamus but inside you know there lies a gentle soul with a soft heart. A Sumo wrestler would make a good buddy to have at your side when the mean streets are at their meanest.

This is a car that looks you in the eye and holds your stare. You don't shove this one around and live to brag about it. It's square shouldered, broad chested, square chinned. It may not be the fastest athlete in the stadium, but its stamina will render it all but unbeatable.

Own a new Range Rover and that's how you'll feel, too. Nobody pushes you around.

If the Range Rover likes you it'll let you inside, its eyes watching you intently all the while as you approach. Pull on the door handle and something that wouldn't be out of place at Fort Knox, swings silently on its

hinges, the leather-scented rush of air cascading after it.

The Range Rover knows its manners, though and has thoughtfully, and oh so discreetly, knelt a little to allow a more elegant entry. The carpets are thick, the leather is soft, the wood and the metals are tactile. The atmosphere in the Range Rover's cabin is intoxicating.

How do you feel? Pampered and privileged.

There's pretty well every gizmo known to motoring man (and woman) in here. The steering wheel can be infinitely positioned with its electric motors – it needs a handbook all of its own to let you in on the secrets of its many switches. The seats move this way and that at the slightest touch of a button.

The centre console is a miracle of technology. Topping it all is a screen that's a TV and a navigation system, a CD player and a radio. This Sumo wrestler knows his way around and will entertain on the trip. There's climate control – it can even sense when

Top: On tarmac the new Range Rover is stable and predictable. Braking power is stupendous. Above: As ever, the Range Rover has a status symbol role to fulfil.

the air outside is more than usually polluted and shuts it out – and there's buttons for more functions than you can take in in one go.

How does it make you feel? Safe, secure, in control.

Those immense doors thud shut. You flick the ignition key – it's in the centre console as the steering lock is way down the column to make forcing it almost impossible. Just one flick of that key, mind. If the ▶

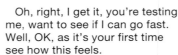

engine needs more than a single crank to fire up, the Range Rover will do that for itself, thank you.

The auto shift looks and feels like a regular stick shift. Click it back into Drive and we're on the move. First impressions are of stunning vision all around, the lightest steering, the easiest touch on the throttle, the sensuality of the seats, the gentle purr of the engine.

This is a vehicle entirely at ease with itself. Its abilities are not to be questioned, but treat it with polite respect and it might show you just a little of what it can do. If you're up to the task yourself, that is.

A gentle saunter through Land Rover's Gaydon complex and the Range Rover gives a muted nod of recognition to the admiring glances. Is that a look of quiet satisfaction on that broad countenance?

There are formalities to complete at the test track security office. The Range Rover waits outside quiet and patient. Take it easy. There's no hurry.

We're on the track and ahead stretches more than a mile of what used to be a runway for V-Bombers back in Cold War days.

We floor the throttle.

Above: Around Land Rover's cross-country test track the Range Rover performs without fuss. The throttle reacts differently off-road, so control is delightfully precise. Below: A curious capacity for holding water. Below right: Not everyone likes the interior styling, but it's sumptuous and thought provoking if nothing else.

Oh, right, I get it, you're testing me, want to see if I can go fast. Well, OK, as it's your first time see how this feels.

The rev counter needle flies, the engine note penetrates the sound deadening for the first time and the Range Rover takes off. Our heads snap back against the high-backed seats and the acceleration just keeps on coming. 70. 80. 90. 100. 110.

The old concrete runway flashes past and in a moment it's time to ease on the brakes for a gentle stop. Hmm, how does that make you feel?

Exhilarated.

We blast back up the runway again. This just keeps getting better.

And back again. This time stand on the brakes at 90 mph. Really stand on them. Hard. We're thrown forward into our seat belts,

the vehicle stopping in what seems micro-seconds. No fuss, no screeching of tyres, no chattering of ABS, no loss of control. Just a short, quick stop. The Range Rover automatically increases the braking effort when it senses an emergency stop taking place.

Straight lines are one thing, of course, but life is full of tricky bends so the Range Rover had better be able to handle them, too. The multi-laned loop that is the main Gaydon test track is smooth tarmac, long straights, a tight bend and a couple of other bends that deceive as they progressively tighten.

When the Range Rover was first introduced into the States in 1987, the Americans went nuts with the wallowing ride comparing the vehicle to a sail boat at sea. Anti-sway bars were rapidly introduced. But that, as they say, is

history and the new Range Rover offers a different prospect altogether.

The need for vastly improved on-road handling has been the driving force behind this latest vehicle's suspension revolution. As you know, there's no separate chassis, no live axles, no coil springs, no rolling, no wallowing, no pitching.

Not surprisingly, this makes the drive an entirely different experience. Passengers no longer rely on the grab handles to stay in their seats, the entire contents of the trinkets tray no longer lands in the driver's lap.

Acceleration is awesome, cornering confident, stopping stupendous. The ride is quiet, smooth, easy. And that makes driver and passengers feel just great.

Easing this motorised hippo round the test track is a joy. The build up of speed excites us as the V8 growls – just enough to let you know that it's doing the business. Steering is light and precise.

Inset: Perfect control through the water – a bow wave over the bonnet is a sign of poor driving. Above: A sight we will no doubt soon be seeing plenty of. Below: Impressive ground clearance and wheel articulation.

The auto box acts just like an auto box should, but slip the lever into what they like to call 'sport' mode and you have manual control back again. Stab the lever back a click and the box shifts down, click it forward and it shifts up. Strange at first not to be stamping your left foot up and down.

It's impossible to tell if Dynamic Stability Control (DSC) is doing anything as you power out of the bends, but it doesn't feel like over or under steering.

It's on the tarmac that the new Range Rover must trounce its rivals and so far our experience is that it has every chance of doing so. Historically the Range Rover has always ▶

been cross-country king and the latest incarnation proves to be no exception to that rule.

There's nothing particularly extreme about Land Rover's off-road test facility at Gaydon, rather it's an intense collection of typical cross-country terrain. If a vehicle fails here it will be through poor driving not mechanical ineptitude.

The water's up to the wheel-larches, the mud is slippy, the climbs and the drops are steep, the side-slopes are scary. All in a day's work, really.

Engaging low box requires slipping the drive into neutral, flicking a switch, then slipping back into

Above: You decide. Similar, but also very different. Below: Don't care much for the door handles or the 'shark gills', but the fascia is lovely and the doors are a work of art in themselves.

drive. DSC needs to be turned off to negotiate some particularly deep and slippery areas – a bit like remembering to engage the centre diff lock, in a way.

No beam axles means no diffs hanging down to plough a furrow down the middle of a track while the wheels follow the ruts. The suspension geometry on each wheel is such that the components have been raised out of harm's way. Overall, the new Range Rover has better ground clearance than the old. And the air suspension works across the axles to provide what you might call virtual axle articulation.

Hill Descent Control gives an

astonishingly low rate of descent on the steepest of hills. Traction control does its stuff on the treacherous climb up the bank out of the water trap.

This is a vehicle that takes care of itself and, in doing so, takes care of its driver and passengers. No matter how bad the conditions, urban or rural, the Range Rover has the equipment and the systems to get through.

The vehicle is truly magnificent. It's a triumph of design and engineering. It's full of character, even quirky in places. Never bland, never ordinary.

And how does that make you feel? Very happy. **LRM**

TEST VEHICLE SPECIFICATIONS		STEERING	
V8 32-valve, aluminium head and block		Rack & pinion steering with Servotronic speed sensitive assistance	
282bhp @ 5400 rpm			
Length/width	4950/2191 mm		
Wheelbase	2880 mm	**TRANSMISSION**	
Track, front/rear	1629/1626 mm	Electronic, dual mode 5-speed automatic gearbox with Steptronic	
Approach angle (Off-road height)	35°	Four-wheel drive system: Two speed chain drive transfer box with	
Departure angle (Off-road height)	29°	Torsen centre differential	
Break over angle (Off-road height)	30°		
Max. ground clearance (Off-road height)	281 mm	Tyres: 255/60 R 18, 255/55 R 19	
Fuel tank capacity	100 litres	Wheels: 7.5 X 18/IS53, 5.5 X 19/IS49, 8.0 X 19/IS57	
Range	617 km (384 miles)		
Weight, unladen - min	2440 kg	0-100 km/h (0-62 mph)	9.2 sec
		Top speed km/h (mph)	208 km/h (130 mph)
Front suspension: Cross-linked electronic air suspension with			
MacPherson air struts		**FUEL CONSUMPTION, EU CYCLE**	
Rear suspension: Cross-linked electronic air suspension with		Urban - ltr/100 km (mpg)	22.2 (12.7)
double wishbones		Extra-urban - ltr/100 km (mpg)	12.6 (22.4)
		Overall - ltr/100 km (mpg)	16.2 (17.4)
		CO_2	389 g/km

THE FACILITIES for this feature were provided by Land Rover at their Gaydon test facility in Warwickshire – PR man Mike Gould presiding. All the British 4x4 and Land Rover magazines were invited to attend – not exactly the 'exclusive' claimed by one.

We began on the braking test straight for, well, brake testing surprisingly enough, and some car-to-car photos. Then we progressed to the test track proper for some high speed circuits to get a feel of the vehicle in motorway type conditions. The weather was appaling but the sense of security inside the Range Rover was remarkable.

What has always made the Range Rover great in all its guises, of course, is its ability to thunder along at high speed, then within moments, be negotiating the trickiest of off-road terrain. And so it is at Gaydon.

Alongside the tarmac track is a carefully crafted off-road evaluation area containing all the kind of things you'd expect – water, mud, ups, downs, sideslopes, craters, ruts, ridges and rocks. Having negotiated our way around that lot for a couple of hours, lunch called, so it was back to Vehicle Operations for the first jet wash of the day, followed by a dousing in the auto wash.

Off to the pub (well you have to, don't you), but getting back was going to be a problem as we were pretty well lost by that time. No worries. Set up the navigation system and the nice lady gave us easy instructions right the way back to the front gate (including a couple of requests to 'make a U-turn if possible).

We wanted a couple of comparison shots against the second generation Range Rover, so Mike got the jet wash out for the second time that day – followed by a second trip through the car wash. As you might imagine, handing back the keys and climbing into the miserable courtesy car that we had been given while our Discovery was in the hospital following a slight on-road coming together, was a disappointment to say the least.

■ Our conclusion was that this is a wonderfully competent vehicle. Clearly designed and engineered by people who care about what they're trying to achieve, some of the detail may not be to everyone's taste, but the basic concept of the new Range Rover is pretty near faultless.

FREE WHEELING

**Was the 2004 Freelander up to scratch?
A test drive through France to Barcelona soon answered the question**

LAND ROVER has an uncanny knack of developing the right vehicle for the market – Range Rover invented the luxury four-wheel drive sector; the Discovery arrived, if a little late to the party, and became the class leader for many years in the full size family market and then came Freelander.

A car without a market segment, we thought at launch, its only rivals being the Toyota Rav 4 and the dowdy Honda Shuttle. Neither had set the sales charts alight nor proven to be a big hit with UK consumers. Land Rover however, had done their homework, spotting consumer preferences shifting towards smaller cars, they decided that a more nimble 4x4 with the style and the ability of a Land Rover would be a big seller, and they were right. Launched at the Frankfurt Motor Show in 1997, Freelander was an instant hit. In its first full year on sale, 1998, some 46,505 were sold and sales have continued to rise with a remarkable 76,599 finding homes in 2002. It quickly established itself as Europe's best selling four wheel

*by
Andy Egerton
photos
Nick Dimbleby*

Nose job. And much better for it – the 2004 Freelander now has a much more intergrated look.

drive and the opposition woke up.

A raft of rivals have arrived on the scene, with still more coming over the next couple of years, Freelander's sales dominance is under threat and for the first time in 2002, Freelander lost the bestseller crown to the Rav 4. Although the car received a comprehensive series of updates in 2001 including new engines, the then new Td4 diesel engine and the fast but thirsty V6, cosmetic changes were kept to a minimum.

So for 2004 Land Rover has instigated a mild freshening of Freelander, aimed at addressing three main areas of complaint; the interior, the frontal appearance of the car and general quality. The question is, is 2004 Freelander a worthy improvement or just a quick nose job to boost stalling sales?

I was keen to find out, and at this point I should reveal that I am something of a Freelander convert. At launch I was a vitriolic skeptic; sure I understood the business case, Land Rover has to make cars consumers want, but was it worthy of the green oval?

Over the last four years Land Rover has worked hard to convince me that my fears were unfounded and my opinion has changed. I like Freelander, it's adept on road, reasonably quick and frugal. But it has had its faults. It looked ugly especially, to my eye, at the front, the minor switch gear was a mess and the overwhelming beigeness of the interior and constant squeaks and rattles from the car whenever I drove one annoyed me.

I was keen to see the new version, and when Land Rover offered me an opportunity to drive one of the first cars off the line, well I just had to say yes. There was a catch however; I had to deliver the car to Southern Spain for them.

On collecting our test car, a Zambesi Silver Td4 SE, the first and most obvious improvement to the 2004 Freelander is to the front. It's very much a case of out with the old and the acres of grey or black plastic which gave the car the look of a beached hippopotamus.

A new front bumper, now body coloured with black inserts and a

mesh grille, gives Freelander a
fresh new stance, positively bold.
Many who saw the car commen-
tated that it looks far more aggressive than the outgoing model.
Revised lights, now twin units that
follow the house style first seen on
the latest Range Rover immediately give Freelander the family
look.

The lights are more than a
cosmetic change however; the
light output is noticeably better
and the additional full beam output
gave reassurance on even the
darkest roads. Our test vehicle was
also fitted with front fog lights, and
again these units impressed with
their brightness and the spread of
light produced.

A new rear bumper follows the
style of the front bumper, body
coloured it gives the car a wider,
more mature stance. The stop-
lights and indicators have moved
into a vertical position in the
bumper sides and having driven a
mixture of dirt roads in all
weathers, it was noticeable just
how little muck they picked up.

But it is in the interior where the
biggest changes have taken place

with major revisions to the seats
and dashboard. Freelander's cabin
has always been a pleasant place
to travel, but for this tester the front
seats have been a disappointment.

With a test route of around 1200
miles to complete, backache
would, on past experience, be a
certainty. However the 2004
Freelander has new front seats,
which utilise seat foams that are
37mm longer under the thighs.
With more leg support there is less
pressure on the lower back, and
the result for this tester, even after
a ten hour stint in the car was a
huge improvement – no back pain.

transmission options
'Les Comos' in Southern Spain
was to be our destination and with
just over two days to reach it we
would have time aplenty to
discover the vices and virtues of
the new Freelander. And one of the
virtues is the Td4 engine. Our test
car also came with the Command-
shift automatic, an ideal combination in my book.

Mechanically the 2004
Freelander is unchanged from the
outgoing model, however Land

*The 'cosmetic' external
changes to the
Freelander have real
benefits, most especially
in improved lighting
front and rear.*

Rover have spent a lot of time and
money over the past couple of
years improving tolerances and
build quality, and it shows.

Around town the Td4 is nippy,
positively peppy in fact, to the
point where passengers are
surprised that it is a diesel. The
changes from the auto box are
smooth and with well chosen ratios
we were able to hold our own in
the cut and thrust of rush hour
traffic in London and the M25. We
crossed the channel via Eurotunnel
and the long drive through France
began.

Once on the Autoroute there was
plenty of time to appreciate the
interior improvements – as noted
the new seats are a huge improvement. The new dashboard
follows the theme first seen in
the Range Rover with strong ▶

vertical aspects and chrome ringed dials. The new dials are clear and the 'chromed' verticals to the binnacle give the dashboard a more contemporary look.

At long last the minor controls for lights are located up on the dash and are now easy to find and operate. On five door cars the electric window switches have at long last moved from their previous awkward location between the seats into the more logical location of the door pulls, which now have a brushed metal finish.

the lady of the dashboard

The final change is the new centre console, which comes with a neat little slot which is the ideal size for your mobile and a revised in car entertainment system. Our test car came with the eight speaker sound system, six CD autochanger and satellite navigation system. The satellite navigation system is a real boon. While waiting to board the

Above: Externally it's the front and rear that show any new features. Internally things are much improved including a Range Rover style central console.

Chunnel train we programmed in Barcelona as our destination. As the unit is built into the radio, the display screen is a little on the small side, but it is very user friendly. We had our destination programmed in, in a matter of minutes and without reference to the comprehensive handbook.

A soothing voice from the dashboard quickly established our current location and advised us we would be getting our feet wet unless we used the train. Smart stuff. Once on the other side of the channel our lady of the dashboard became a faithful companion and was unerringly accurate in her countdown to a change of directions.

However, as we received our next set of directions from her sitting in the main square of Orange in southern France, a momentous flash of lightning caused the system to quit mid sentence. Maybe she just didn't like the thunder storm and hid under the dashboard. In fairness this particular storm made the national and international news for

its severity, and that particular bolt of lightening did little for our mobile phones either.

This was the first time I had used the channel tunnel, and it was an excellent way to cross to France, almost a non-event. Drive on and forty-five minutes later you are leaving the train and hitting the autoroute.

Freelander has always been a good car on the road, revisions to the dampers and suspension made in 2001 improved the ride and made the steering more taut and responsive. Not much has changed for 2004, all the attributes are still there and on the billiard table smooth French autoroutes the ride was a joy.

With the cruise control set to 130 kph, the air conditioning keeping the severe heat of a French summer at bay, it was time to settle back and enjoy the view. The Td4 was turning over at an indicated 2700rpm and proving to be relatively frugal, returning a figure of around 35 miles to every gallon.

We crossed the border into

Spain and the weather took a turn for the worse, a darkly oppressive sky was broken by flashes of lightning that are seemingly only to be found in mountainous areas. With the rain now coming in hard, so hard the wipers could barley clear the screen, the Freelander remained sure footed, the standard fit Michelin tyres on 17 inch alloy wheels were giving plenty of grip, but as the volume of standing water increased even they were beginning to struggle and, as we felt the car begin to wiggle occasionally, we felt it was time to exercise a little discretion and pulled into a rest halt.

Turning off the autoroute it was time to see how Freelander coped with the rigours of back road Spain. The tight and often twisty mountainous roads proved the handling of Freelander, which is good. The rack and pinion steering is nicely weighted and gives good communication to just how hard the tyres are having to work. With a good lock, manoeuvring Freelander around the narrow confines of some of the towns we passed through was easy, the power steering making light of the demands.

The mountain roads also showed the Td4 Freelander's one weakness, a lack of power. When the opportunities came to overtake the lumbering wagons climbing over the mountains, the Freelander was slow to pickup and I felt it was struggling. The five speed Jatco automatic gearbox is a smooth unit, and proved willing to drop down a cog when it felt it was needed. Using the Command Shift option improves things a little, the ability to move down a cog or even two when you feel the car begin to labour is a useful option.

It's a shame that Land Rover did not take this opportunity to give Freelander a bit more power, reprogramming the engine management for another 30 brake horsepower would transform the car, giving it the extra grunt it so obviously needs and can handle. With our destination in sight it was time to try Freelander's other

Above: Rear end looks much neater and the 2004 Freelander still proves highly competent off the tarmac.

party piece.

The track up to Les Comos, a beautiful hacienda in the mountains behind Barcelona, was wet, muddy and slippery. The thunder storm we had encountered, had also passed through this area leaving the ground sodden. Freelander coped with it all. The four wheel-drive and dual purpose Michelins got us through. But then that's the beauty of Freelander, an effortless drive; smooth, comfortable, nippy and quick on the road and then an ability to handle rough stuff that would leave many of its competitors gasping.

Land Rover has worked hard with Freelander, constant updates have seen it evolve and mature into a good little car. The latest tweaks solve most of the remaining gripes that most of us had with it, and will help Freelander to stay competitive in the most aggressive sector of the four wheel drive market. As I said, I like Freelander, I like the 2004 model even more. **LRM**

MEMORY LANES

Three well-travelled vehicles team up once again in Wales to revisit some classic lanes in the company of a pair of trail bikes

by
Jenny Morgan

OLD LAND Rovers never die. They just get recycled, so they say. So often a tired vehicle is lovingly restored, the owner taking the opportunity to modify their creation to more suit their needs while retaining the core values inherent in such a machine; while others are passed on through the hands of subsequent enthusiasts, more often retaining a character all of their own that leads the new owner down familiar paths.

Certainly our four wheeled companions for this trip have such a history, whether that be a ground-up restoration to rival grandad's broom, or simply passed

Below left: Jenny Morgan on bike, followed by TEW, Baby and Tango.
Below right: Tango takes a dive – water is plentiful in central Wales.

on through the hands of enthusiastic off-road drivers. All three will be familiar to regular readers of the Land Rover press over the years.

Wales has always offered the off-road enthusiast a wealth of diverse terrain, solitude, and a little adventure, while not being a million miles away from home. The perfect destination for a long weekend away with friends, enjoying the warm hospitality of the local people and the magnificence of nature's more dramatic work on the British Isles.

Indeed, in more recent years, we have seen a number of businesses thriving in the area which positively encourage and promote responsible use of the green lane network. The more independent traveller (which I consider myself to be) has welcomed the active participation of many of the local authorities to retain and maintain the byway network for all user groups to enjoy.

With this in mind, and with the Easter bank holiday weekend fast approaching, it was my intention to spend a few days away – and it just so happened that a handful of other **LRM** staff and contributors had similar ideas.

return to roots

Having jetted all over Europe recently on the Range Rover Sport launch, **LRM** photographer and contributor Nick Dimbleby was itching to get back to what inspired him to work with Land Rovers in the first place. Together with wife Lisa, he is no stranger to off-roading in Wales in their very tidy 100 inch Hybrid 'TEW'. However, other than the odd randonee event, the majority of the time Nick spends in Wales is working, so this time it would really be for fun – although thankfully, he also

brought his cameras along.

So, too, our seemingly desk-bound Editor had got itchy feet – having spent the last few years reading about everyone else out having a good time. He recently bought back his old Defender 200Tdi 'Tango' from contributor Andy Cutting, and was keen to get back to explore a region he last visited more than a dozen years ago, behind the wheel of that very same vehicle. Although no stranger to off-roading, Richard's wife (and

LRM Production Director) Cathie, was also keen to see just what the mythical Wales had to offer.

The final vehicle in our four-wheeled trio is perhaps the most (in)famous Land Rover of them all when it comes to Wales. 'Baby' was christened by the late Tim Webster. As a regular contributor to Richard's previous publication, Tim was one of the pioneering writers about greenlaning in the UK, and spent much of his free time exploring (at that time) little

From left (above): Cathie, Rich, Nick, Moira and Dom – Photo by Lisa. Below: Magnificent isolation, a perfect spot for a picnic and one of the reasons that makes green lane driving so appealing.

known routes across the country, with Wales and the border regions being his favourite destination.

Indeed, Tim's pioneering spirit meant he often travelled alone, with only his V8 and Warn winch to get him out of any trouble – which it must be said, he found himself in on quite a number of occasions. Certainly, Tim's writing inspired many people to follow in his foot-steps, and his many hours of research in local authority archives has paid dividends ▶

to all those who currently utilise many old roads that had once been forgotten, and prompted others to fight for the right to retain the use of motorised vehicles on appropriate rights of way.

Tim's Land Rover was passed on to long time friend and off-roading companion Dave Lane, whose adventures with his compatriots have become the stuff of legend – from dune jumping in the Sahara desert to greenlaning in a 101FC amongst others, and remained in his hands for many years. The current owner is now Dominic Marder (with his wife Moira), a marketing consultant, who is also responsible for the success of the **LRM** show at Gaydon each year.

Although the D90 was still is sound condition, Dominic has seen fit to install a number of modifica-

TEW leads the way on Strata Florida. This deep water crossing proved to be one of the most memorable spots of the trip.
Below: Two V8s and a 200Tdi, unkindly referred to by the petrolheads as a tractor, but it made less visits to the filling stations.

tions (including a 3.9-litre Efi V8 and Detroit locking differentials), while retaining the simplicity of the original vehicle. Tim would have been proud.

one-wheel-drive

As I have been spending far more time on two wheels recently, I thought it would be fun to take the bike along to show the others how off-roading compares on two versus four wheels. There are plus and minus points to either – of course, four-wheel-drive offers vastly superior traction. However, fundamentally, the (lack of) size and weight of an off-road motor-cycle gives you much more manoeuvrability and choice of line when negotiating hazards.

Also, competition derived suspension means the ride over rough ground is like a magic carpet when compared to even the most supple coil-sprung Land Rover. You do get wetter, though. My friend Julie was more than keen to join us on her bike too – and although relatively new to off-roading, she is an accomplished rider and completely taken with the adventure aspect that green lane riding/driving provides.

early starters

So, at the crack of dawn as we trailered the bikes into the middle of Wales, the Land Rover contin-gent were already tucking into a hearty breakfast before embarking on a few lanes prior to our rendezvous at midday. Rather fortunately, the timing of our trip coincided with the period that one of the most famous lanes in South Wales is open to traffic, being under a TRO (Traffic Regulation

Order) for all but a month in the spring and again in the autumn.

Although the majority of this particular route has a hard stone surface, this road is usually closed to vehicular traffic in an effort to preserve the road from unnecessary damage due to over-use.

Thankfully, this is respected by user groups so that the route may continue to be used by all of us. And it is this very kind of compromise that should be encouraged between user groups and local authorities, rather than see lanes closed indefinitely though inaccurate reclassification to bridleway, for example.

The plan for our weekend was to take in a few favourite lanes, some familiar to all of us, others new to the four wheeled contingent, and all new to Dominic and Moira in the blue 90 – although, of course, like a

faithful St. Bernard, I imagine those wheels will recall many of the lanes in the hands of its previous owners.

As such, I was primarily in charge of plotting a suitable route, minimising the amount of time spent on-road, but at the same time, taking in some of the more dramatic scenery in the region, tarmac or not.

After all, it is the very nature of 'all-terrain' vehicles that allow us the freedom to explore either on road or off, and this was meant to be a holiday. We were not out to test ourselves unduly, After all, the majority of green lanes are essentially 'rough roads' rather than competition style stages anyway, and the environment needs to be respected.

However, the nature of Welsh byways is that you often come across a tricky section – either

Top left: High centred on a stump, the hi-lift raises Tango just enough to allow the 90 to be driven free.
Top right: TEW fords another river in the shadow of one of the region's most impressive dams.
Above left to right: At least Cathie seems to know which way to go; respect for the countryside is essential; heating up a can of V8 juice on the Tdi's exhaust manifold (it really works); Ms Morgan struggles.

through weather erosion, or the ever present soft and boggy ground prevalent between rocky outcrops. As such, we were reasonably well prepared, two of the three Land Rovers had winches (Dominic even had a demountable one for the rear), and a selection of ropes, shackles and strops.

Two other important pieces of equipment are bridging/bog ladders, and a ground anchor of some kind – none of which they were carrying – however, having recce'd the route barely a month before, I was confident the Land Rovers would have little trouble on our proposed journey.

So, as we headed off on our wild adventure, the sky uncharacteristically blue for so early in the year, each of us were to have our own favourite memories of the trip. *Jenny Morgan* ▶

MOTORBIKES? WHAT on earth are they doing in **LRM** magazine? Well, let me tell you people, off-roading on two wheels takes on a whole new dimension. The intimacy you experience by being one step closer to the elements means every sight, sound and smell is even more intense than in an open-topped Land Rover, it just hurts more if you fall off.

Of course, the British motorcycle industry being what it is, one really has to look to the east if you want a serious off-road motorcycle, and the Honda XR400 is renowned the world over as a 'classic' trail bike. To draw a four-wheeled analogy, it can, perhaps, be be likened to a trail prepped Defender 90, fitted with a honking great diesel engine and Old Man Emu suspension – old school, but a pretty damn near bullet proof combination that should prove ultra reliable.

Meanwhile, Julie's KTM is of Austrian origin, and essentially the very latest full-on Enduro race bike – more akin to a Bowler Wildcat with a 5-litre TVR engine, and coil-over shocks – but still eminently suitable for green laning. Despite their racy appearances, both these bikes differ from their motocross counterparts in that they are fully road-legal, and can be ridden quite considerable distances if required.

Overlanding on a bike certainly teaches you how to pack light. We endeavoured to remain self-sufficient during the trip, so kit was shared between our rucksacks.

Perhaps the best illustration of the difference between two and four wheels was the deep river crossing on the second day - without the facility of a snorkel, a bike is really limited to a wading depth of around three feet, and a bumpy riverbed does not help traction or stability. Conversely, we were able to ride around tree stumps, rocks and gullies that had the Land Rovers hooked up for ages. Viva la difference.
Jenny Morgan

Julie takes an early bath – in March the water that floods from the mountains is cold – really cold.

WAY BACK, way, way back, in the early nineties, H20 LRM was a regular on the LRO Challenges in north Wales, when I edited that magazine. The registration number was different then, of course, and she had a hard top with windows and bench seats in the back.

She led a very adventurous life,

Cathie's eye view, as Baby follows, deep inside the glorious Welsh countryside.
Right: Dominic operates the hi-lift to raise Tango's front diff over a stump.

once ending up on her side in a seriously deep roadside ditch, suffering a bent con rod after the engine 'hydraulicked' in muddy water; bending and scraping just about every panel in Wales and elsewhere, bellied out, cross axled and trialed at local and national level. In short, she was well-used

and not a little abused.

What a way to treat a 90, but it's all character building stuff and Tango, as she has come to be known, lapped it all up and came back for more. But then it was time for us to get sensible, and we replaced Tango with a Discovery. She went off ▶

deeper into the wilds of Suffolk to enjoy more off-road trips and even an expedition to North Africa in the capable ownership of **LRM** writer Andy Cutting.

But now Andy has set his sights on bigger things and is refurbishing a 110, so Tango has come back home, sporting a black canvas top, swingaway wheelcarrier and Volvo seats. Her winch, though, is literally a basket case – David Bowyer where are you, we need help.

Her first trip out with us just had to be back to Wales, so we fitted a set of Silverline modular wheels and

Hancook Mud Terrains to get her around a bit better and off we went.

The 200Tdi with its Jeremy Fearn intercooler still pulls well, though I think the turbocharger may be on the way out. With a couple of new dampers and a thorough service, she was back up to standard again, and what a joy to get back behind the wheel of a 90 and explore some of the very familiar classic lanes of mid-Wales.

The greatest advantage of using an older vehicle off-road is that you

Below: A vehicle with more history than the British Museum. TEW started life as a Range Rover, then became the hybrid that influenced rock star Bryan Adams, before being transformed once again by photographer Nick Dimbleby.

don't mind so much about the scratches from trees and bushes, attacks from tree stumps and masses of mud and goo piling up under the chassis.

Things to do? Repair or replace the winch; fit more underbody protection, tidy up the dash, maybe get a Mobile Storage System cubby box and load bay draw. Locking diffs? Perhaps. Suspension lift? Most definitely.

Watch this space, as they say.
Richard Howell-Thomas

AS YOU can hopefully see from the photographs that accompany this feature, Wales is a beautiful place. I've been coming here to photograph its stunning land-scape (more often than not with a Land Rover) ever since I got my driving license, and the fact that it boasts some of the best off-roading in the country is a great bonus, too.

My introduction to Wales was in the company of the late, great Tim Webster, when I participated in the 'Rebecca Riots' off-road expedition in the autumn of 1991. As I didn't own a Land Rover at that time, I passengered with Tim in his normally-aspirated 90 diesel pick-up. During that time, his enthusiasm for Wales, its off-roading, its scenery and its history was infectious, and I've been hooked ever since.

Over the past 14 years I've been fortunate enough to drive most of the 'classic' off-road tracks – some once, some numerous times – and each one has fond memories attached to it. These were made by the people I was with, the banter in the bar, the vehicle I was driving (a real assortment ranging from my own Land Rover, TEW, to an £80,000

Range Rover Autobiography), and can be recalled from the photographs that are squirreled away in my archive, or by simply driving the track again a few years later.

Of course, many of the lanes have changed over that time – some for the better, some for the worse; although on our trip over Easter, I was saddened to see large patches of land having been forested. Some areas, particularly on Strata Florida, have been changed almost beyond recognition, and I just hope that a replanting programme is in operation.

Other tracks are now closed for much of the year (The Gap Road near Brecon for example), while others have a permanent TRO placed on them. I feel lucky to have been able to drive them when I did.

Let's hope that the lanes that do remain stay open for the enjoyment of all users now and in the future, so that I can, in turn, introduce others to the beauty of Wales in the same way that Tim Webster did for me all those years ago.

Enjoy the photos.
Nick Dimbleby

I'VE OWNED 'Baby' for about two years and have enjoyed every minute of it. Baby was bought from Dave Lane who owned it for about 13 years – previously it was owned by Tim Webster, which is where its name comes from. As with many Land Rovers, Baby has had various incarnations but has remained a Land Rover used for what it was built for – off-roading.

For months I had been thinking about visiting Wales and how great it would be to spend a weekend just exploring the classic lanes such as the Gap road or Strata Florida. You could say it would be a nostalgic trip for Baby (as this is where Dave and Tim spent so much time with the Land Rover), and a new experience for me.

In the short time I've owned the vehicle, modifications have been added from jackable sills to more rugged off-road tyres. With all my modifications, I wished to improve the off-road capability without going too crazy.

Axle articulation has always been a favourite of mine, I've seen some really radical kits that make you gasp as well as various 'off the shelf' spring and shock kits that are easy to fit at home. Ultimately, what I wanted was something that simply hugged the terrain and kept me going through the toughest of conditions. There are various radical suspension kits on the market but, after numerous emails and phone conversations, I settled for a trip up to Tomcat Motorsport.

The decision came to me like a bolt of lightening, why do I need to have such radical axle articulation when a set of long travel shocks, some new springs and a set of Detriot diffs could do the job for about the same price? Quite simply, you're most likely to have at least two wheels on the ground, with enough traction to get through.

Tomcat had the springs custom made for the vehicle to maximise travel without sacrificing too much. I chose a Detriot torque bias diff for the front and a Detroit locker for the rear, reducing the risk of breaking the half shafts on the front axle, but with plenty of traction all round.

There was, however, one thing I really wanted to do to Baby before we hit Wales – an engine change. Ever since I sold my Range Rover Classic a couple of years ago, I've really missed the 3.9 Efi. Baby had always been a 3.5 V8 90 with the original Santana gearbox, but I wanted engine refinement, so that's what I got.

After searching for a suitable engine, I went to Yattendon Garage, with one engine in the front and one in the back. Bob, the proprietor, and I discussed exactly how they were to fit the new block, particularly focusing on the ancillary components of the 3.9.

Moira, my wife, and I, had never been off-roading together before, because cars simply do not interest her – something I still cannot understand to this day. But, during the Easter trip, she happily sat in the passenger seat marvelling at the breathtaking views and began to really appreciate Baby's capabilities.

Having been virgins to Wales, we couldn't get over how beautiful this country truly is. Each and every lane had its own character, providing not only challenging terrain but located in the most tranquil area of the country we have ever seen.

Baby could not have performed any better, crossing bogs, climbing steep ravines and winching the odd vehicle or two. Though come to think of it, she did stall in the first river crossing, a gentle reminder that, while you may have all the right kit, Mother Nature can still have her way.

Dominic Marder

BY INCLUDING the bikes in this feature, we hope to illustrate to all responsible green lane users that there should be no conflict between different user groups, regardless of how many wheels (or, indeed, feet or hooves) they employ. We believe this is particularly important for the motorised vehicle communities, as it is only by working together and providing a united front that we can hope to convince the current Government bodies to reassess their proposals to close down much of the green lane network currently in use.

Both LARA (Land Access & Recreation Association) and the TRF (Trail Riders Fellowship) are working together with other motor vehicle user groups to retain these rights for all of us, and we urge you to support them wherever you can.

Indeed, what this trip proved to all of us, is just what enjoyment can be had by using vehicles on appropriate rights of way. We were able to picnic on the edge of a hidden lake at over 1,000ft elevation, yet barely half a mile from the coast.

We were immersed in the shady solitude of lush pine forests, and watched the sun go down over vast reservoirs and craggy peaks. We revelled in the ability to see parts of the countryside that few would even imagine were there or ever think to visit, viewed rare wildlife in their natural surroundings, undisturbed by our presence, then enjoyed evenings of warm hospitality in a local hotel who were

Opposite page: Wheel travel with a vengeance. Inset above: Waders Cottage. Below: The Gap.

happy to accommodate our muddy boots and weary faces.

We, in turn, supported the local community to the tune of over £1,000 during the weekend, with food, fuel, accommodation and, not least, a flagon or two of ale.

Albeit brief, it was a trip I'm sure we will all remember for a very long time. A series of magic moments – some physical, others emotional – shared amongst like minded others with a passion for the countryside and adventure.

It was, of course, by no means unique to ourselves, no doubt many of you have had similar experiences too – and long may we have the opportunity for those to continue.

Jenny Morgan

LRM

It's summer 2000 and the Range Rover is still 'a car for
all reasons' says Andy Egerton as he brings together...

...SOMETHING OLD
AND SOMETHING NEW

MANUFACTURED BY
THE ROVER Co LTD
SOLIHULL ENGLAND

RANGE ROVER

CHASSIS Nº 355000 03A

MAX VEHICLE LADEN WT.	5520 LBS.	2504 Kg.
MAX FRONT AXLE WT.	2200 LBS.	998 Kg.
MAX REAR AXLE WT.	3320 LBS.	1506 Kg.

BY
**LAND
ROVER**

THERE SHE sat in a quiet corner of the garage. All alone, unlike the others who were being fussed over and pampered, seemingly incongruous amongst all the other stars. And yet she is a star, nay, dare one say, an icon. She fundamentally changed people's perceptions, created a whole new genre and thirty years later she is still the benchmark against which others like to judge themselves. We are, of course, talking about the Range Rover which, just in case it's escaped your attention, is currently celebrating its 30th anniversary. And our particular star? YVB 153H The very first production specification Range Rover to come off the line in 1969.

The fact that YVB became the first example to come off the line is as much a quirk of fate as any other. It was just one of a batch of twenty eight pre-production prototypes. These were built on the newly installed production line at Solihull and would be used by the engineering teams to validate the build process, identify problems and train assembly line staff. All of the twenty eight vehicles were to be allocated production chassis numbers. Roger Crathorne who was a junior engineer on the project, kindly looked up his

records for me and they reveal some interesting asides. What became YVB 153H was scheduled for build on 26 November, 1969 and was originally planned to be painted Amazon Green. Planned as vehicle number three it was allocated chassis number 003A and should have been the third vehicle to come off the line. At the last moment it was decided to paint it Tuscan Blue. That one decision sealed its fate and its place in history.

Rover's publicity department was planning a promotional film called 'A Car for All Reasons' and preparing for brochure photography. They planned to use vehicles painted red and white, however the photographer requested a blue one in place of the white as this would be more photogenic.

Consequently, as YVB was the only blue vehicle then under construction, its build was accelerated with the vehicle coming off the line on 17 December, 1969. Geof Miller, who was Project Engineer for development of the Range Rover, remembers that they had to tow the vehicle off the line part finished, there were no production specification seats and trim parts available. After a spell in the engineering section, YVB emerged fully trimmed to production spec and was

by
Andy Egerton

Today's Range Rovers have their ancestry firmly rooted with the first models launched more than thirty years ago. Recognisably similar, but vastly different in style and specification, the earliest and the latest models make for a fascinating comparison.

released to the sales department on 26 January, 1970.

press launch

Roger remembers that they took the vehicle to Beddgelert in Wales for the press pictures to be taken, and after its starring role in the launch publicity, it was returned to the engineering fleet and was used for further development work as well as being used by Land Rover engineering supremo Tom Barton. Regularly used by the company's directors as a demonstrator, it was eventually sold on 12 January, 1972 to William Ellis Garages, a Rover dealer in Shropshire.

Thirty years on and there sits YVB in a quiet corner of the workshop at the Heritage Motor Centre, fresh from her starring role in the anniversary celebrations and a recent turn at the Royal Show. Even today the design still looks fresh; instantly recognisable. The world may have moved on and customers today have much higher expectations, but it's easy to see why the type caused such a stir when it was launched. The first thing to hit you are the doors, just how incredibly large and heavy they are. They shut with the kind of clunk you get from a safe door, giving an almost tank-like quality.

A little choke and the ▶

engine fires first time and settles into a soft burble so distinctive of V8s. The chaps in the workshop warn me that she has been a little temperamental of late and she may well break down. Nothing could be further from the truth, throughout the day she started first time every time and never failed to please. But I'm getting ahead of myself here.

Reversing out of the workshop brings the next revelation, the steering. With no power assistance a three point turn becomes a biceps building experience, the 'armstrong' system comes to the fore. Heading out of the museum it's the steering wheel which I notice most. It's incredibly thin and hard on the hands, but as we gather speed the steering lightens up and by comparison with many Range Rovers I've driven, remarkably direct around the straight

Above: A motoring icon. The Range Rover is still regarded by many as the definitive luxury off-road model. Planned as vehicle number three, YVB was allocated chassis number 003A and should have been the third vehicle to come off the line.

ahead. I can't help but smile as we drive around the grounds of the Heritage Centre. The vehicle still pulls remarkably well, the engine is smooth and flexible, a poke of the loud pedal reveals she's still capable of spirited acceleration. Fortunately the brakes are as good today as when the car was launched, the big discs all round provide plenty of stopping power.

eye-opener

In deference to Heritage's wishes and the expected breakdown, we don't stray too far and make the most of the centre's tracks. After a few laps I'm beginning to feel at home. The clutch is heavy, far more so than I remember, but it's the gear shift that's the eye opener. A huge great wand of a gear lever attached to a basic four-speed box and a throw-action

that in normal circumstances would win me an Olympic javelin medal. Slow and positive would seem to be the best way forward, the cogs go in nice and easily and there's no clunks from the drive train. Remarkable in a vehicle that's as old as this.

Parking up to take pictures and it's time to take stock. YVB is starting to look its age, the Tuscan Blue paintwork is beginning to peel in places and there are signs of past touch ups. The wheels have been repainted silver rather than the correct gunmetal and the tailgate is refusing to close properly. Inside, the story is much the same The vinyl seats, with their distinctive three fingers of a Kit-Kat appearance are split and sagging. The headlining, always a troublesome area, is beginning to sag alarmingly, the dash has some screw holes

where there really shouldn't be any and the paint on the steering wheel has worn away. All are sure signs of the hard life it has endured in the past. But these are things that give it personality and one of the things that gave the original Range Rover so much of its personality was its engine.

Lifting the bonnet was the next revelation. It is incredibly heavy. Is this normal, I wonder? There in the engine bay sits the lovely little Rover V8. It looks so at home here and for those of us brought up on today's high tech, emission regulated units the lack of piping, trunking and wiring gives it an almost quaint charm. But there again, the world was a different place thirty years ago.

I'd argue that there are five truly great motoring icons, cars which defined their particular market segments and re-wrote the way

we thought about that type of vehicle.

The Porsche 911 series is still one of the truly great sports cars, instantly recognisable and a benchmark against which others are judged.

The original Volkswagen Beetle still looks good today and is still in limited production. Forget the new Beetle, it's a pastiche, a worthless bit of kitsch and a fashion accessory.

The Mini, revolutionised the way cars were driven with front wheel drive. It's still the definitive town car and great fun to drive. Will the new Mini be as good? We will have to wait and see, though I fear it may, like the new Beetle, be just a pastiche.

not one, but two
Then we come to Land Rover. Most manufacturers would be

Above: One area where YVB scores a convincing win over the current model is the rear end treatment, it has a more coherent appearance than the current design. Above centre: The Rover V8 looks so at home here and for those of us brought up on today's high tech, emission regulated units, the lack of piping, trunking and wiring gives it an almost quaint charm.

happy to have one icon, let alone two. The Defender is still the definitive 4x4, bedrock of the company and the Swiss Army Knife of the four wheel drive world. Every bit as capable today as it was back in 1948, park today's Defender next to the original model and the lineage is there for all to see. Then we have Range Rover, still regarded by many as the definitive luxury off-road model. Eminently capable as a luxury sedan or as a mud plugger. The Range Rover didn't just redefine the four wheel drive market, it created a whole new market.

Replacing such a ground breaking vehicle was always going to be difficult. Change it too much and the enthusiasts would be howling in protest, too little and the charge would be of conservatism. Remember the fuss at the time of the ▶

second generation's launch. Had Land Rover gone too far? Or maybe not far enough? Six years on and it would be fair to say that they got it just about right. Designed to have a model life of eight years it will be coming up to that anniversary when its successor makes an appearance. It says much for the integrity of the design that it has lasted this long without the need for a facelift or major changes to enhance sales.

tough comparison

Choosing a vehicle to compare with the original model would on paper appear be a simple task, a base model with a 4.0 V8 with manual transmission would, in theory, be the most appropriate. Mechanically most certainly, however, we must remember that at its launch the Range Rover was touted as a luxury vehicle. So, after much debate in the **LRM**

Back in 1970 the Range Rover was designed as a 'posh' Land Rover and it was felt that a plastic coated interior would cope best with muddy boots and be capable of being hosed out occasionally. Today's Range Rover makes no such assumptions or concessions, with its deep pile carpets, rouched leather trim and a full wood kit.

office, we decided that the 2000 model year Autobiography represents the pinnacle of the current model and would make the most interesting comparison. Parking the two of them together was quite a revealing experience.

It says much for the purity of the original King and Bashford creation that the current model draws upon it so much. The unmistakable styling cues are all there. The castelated bonnet, the gently sloping split rear tailgate and the swage line down the flanks all are carried on to the 'new' model. One area where YVB scores a convincing win over the current model is the rear end treatment, even without black rear quarter panels which give it an almost naked appearance, it still has a more coherent appearance than the current design.

The interior is perhaps the area of greatest contrast. Back in 1970 vinyl was the height of luxury in

automotive interiors, coming in standard, deluxe and super deluxe formats in most everyday cars. The Range Rover was designed as a 'posh' Land Rover and consequently it was felt that a plastic coated interior would cope best with muddy boots, the odd pig and be capable of being hosed out occasionally. Today's Range Rover makes no such assumptions or concessions. With deep pile carpets, rouched leather trim and a full wood kit, no muddy boots will probably ever see the interior of most of today's vehicles. The dash too is an area of major contrast. YVB has a simple binnacle with a speedo, water temperature and fuel gauge - that's all. No pretensions to cutting edge technology. At the time of its launch, man had just taken his first steps on the moon. The current Range Rover has more available computing power in just its engine management

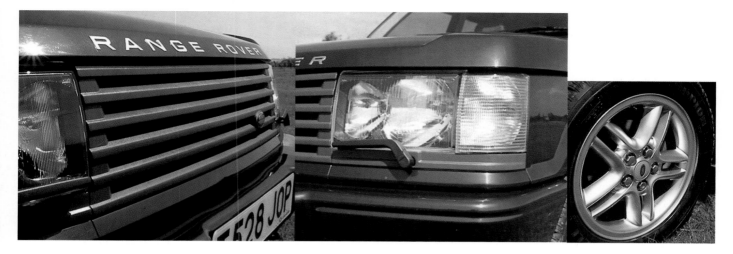

system than NASA had for the moon shots.

There is no shortage of gizmos and toys on today's vehicle: air suspension, electric memory seats, satellite navigation system, CD and video system, to name but a few. How many we really need is a different matter, but in the market segment that Range Rover now competes, customers expect and want such items. Or is it merely a reflection of the technological times in which we live. I wonder.

each to his own

So which is the best, the original simple model or today's all singing all dancing model? It's more a case of what I would be doing with the vehicle. If I was going off to the remotest jungles of South America then the original model would be the preferred choice. Its bog simple engineering and ease of repair marks it out. But there are

few truly remote areas left in the world and those there are, the local people all drink Coca-Cola, have mobile phones and wear Nike training shoes.

Thirty years on the world is now a global village, international air travel has shrunk the world and even the remotest of locations is contactable thanks to satellite communications. We have become a technology based society and today's Range Rover reflects that change. Its 4.0 V8, now in its twilight years, still gives ample performance and is a lovely, sweet little unit. The ride is superb and the handling, if not quite as good as some of the current class leaders, is still respectable. The interior appointments are hard to fault. If I had to cross Europe in a hurry, then this would be my choice.

The fact is I like them both. The original model exudes a charisma that in no small part contributed

to its success and it's not difficult to see why it caused such a sensation when it was launched. Today's model is eminently practical as everyday transport and every bit as capable in the rough as the original. Thirty years on and still a 'car for all reasons', here's to the next thirty... **LRM**

Above: The availability of new materials and technologies has led to vastly different shapes and lines, particularly noticeable at the front end.

Below: Inside, the P38A Range Rover simply reeks of leather-bound opulence and prosperity, while being packed with all the toys that an owner could want.

■ THANKS TO Roger Crathorne and Geof Miller for taking the time to look through their records and answer my questions, and special thanks to the Heritage Motor Centre at Gaydon in Warwickshire for the loan of YVB.

The museum has more than 350 vehicles on display at any one time. The centre is located just off Junction 12 of the M40 and is open throughout the year. Telephone 01926 641188 for more information.

WHAT CAN I GET FOR

£2,500?

Older vehicles only in this price range, but there are plenty of good ones to be found – be prepared to spend time searching for the best

FOR £2,500 we set out to find a good, solid, dependable Land Rover, the sort that will work hard for you all day long, but not cost a fortune to maintain and repair. Although there are some good examples of older Range Rovers and Discoverys to be found at this price, they don't really fall into the workhorse category, so we dismissed those. A 90 or 110 is an obvious candidate but to get a really good one you probably need to spend a bit more, and £2,500 was the limit of our budget.

A Series III seemed the best choice and without too much effort we found the brilliant example for sale at Landys of Bury St Edmunds. It's an ex-military 109 civilian pattern (CL) vehicle and was probably used for liason work, by the TA or on an RAF base. Its condition suggests it has been in store or at least used in the dry somewhere.

Though this is a genuine ex-military, don't let a fresh coat of NATO matt green lead you into thinking any such vehicle is. There will be a discrepancy on the registration document as it will have been used under a military number. This one has an age related number current when made or first used, and will state declared made in 1982.

It stands up well and is level with none of the characteristic sagging to one side. All the panels look original and the odd gentle bruise is better than a load of new panels that might hide any previous hard use.

Do not set your heart on a vehicle as good as this – it is exceptionally good and a rare find.

VIN plate

THE VIN number plate in this vehicle is on the back of the bulkhead. On older Series IIIs, it is on the front panel just in front of the battery on the left side. The number should correspond to the one on the registration document and was originally punched in the chassis on the outside of the front right hand spring hanger, just above the spring mounting bolt. A replacement front outrigger will delete this, so not finding it is not a major cause for concern. Being an ex-military vehicle it might have another VIN plate on the seat box outer edge visible with the door open. It might also have its previous forces number on it.

All chassis numbers can be decoded and lists are published in workshop manuals or on the internet. Being post-1979 when VINS came out in the current form this one ought to start SALL-BCAH1AA followed by its serial number. It translates as a 109 four cylinder petrol RHD with four speed box built at Solihull.

Look at other age clues on the vehicle. This one has anti-burst door locks, removable section on the bulkhead in front of the gearlever, late seventies rear bumperettes and push on door seals confirming its age. If it were a bit newer it would have one up and one down lights on the rear like a 110 and a plastic Land Rover badge. Of course, all these might have been changed especially on a rebuilt vehicle.

This one is probably quite safe but be especially vigilant with pre-1973 ones that enjoy a tax free status, as many are newer vehicles on old log books.

OUR CHOICE

winch

THIS VEHICLE has a Fairy Mechanical drum winch. It is doubtful if it is an original fitment, but at about £300 secondhand, is another bonus feature. Being mechanically driven, it is reliable and you can winch all day without flattening the battery. The power for it comes from the PTO hole in the back of the gearbox and it would not be possible to fit an overdrive as well. Don't pay extra if it will be unused and sit as a rusting heavy lump of metal on the bumper. It also makes the steering heavier. Check the wire cable before you use it for rust and fraying. If unsure of its operation get expert tuition in its use.

door tops

THIS VEHICLE has the bonus of having aluminium door tops as used on early 110s and currently on military vehicles. They do not rot like the steel ones and the front window opens as well. Being as they fit in the same two holes they often turn up on vehicles that predate their use, and especially on ex-military ones. As they fetch £200, or even more for a pair second hand, it is a real attraction to this vehicle. The original steel ones are prone to rotting but only cost £45 complete with glass or £18 without. While it is a positive attribute to have good ones, rotten ones are no problem to sort out as long as the price reflects it.

bulkhead

THOUGH PRONE to corrosion in the steel bulkhead corners, this one is original and good. There is no evidence of corrosion. The original spot welds and seam welding is clearly visible so it has not been repaired by welding or body filler. For a 23-year-old bulkhead it is really good. Removing the top hinge and spraying in wax-oyl regularly will help it stay this way.

Welding repairs with proper repair sections are alright if done properly, i.e. the rust cut out completely and new metal let in to fill the gap and welded to sound original material. Too often the repair sections are just fitted to cover over the corrosion which soon breaks out again. Following repairs again wax through the hole into the bulkhead behind the hinge will help corrosion repairs last longer but replacement is inevitable in the long term.

hand throttle

BEING MILITARY this petrol Land Rover has a hand throttle. It is not designed for high speed motorway cruising, but for speeding up the tickover if standing, ticking over with the lights on or heater running. On this vehicle it will also be useful with the winch. Diesels have one as standard to give a smoother high tick over in cold engine conditions.

footwell

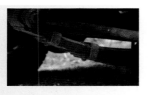

REPLACEMENT FOOTWELLS are available for both sides and if welded in properly are a satisfactory repair. The replacements do not have the ridges in them you can see here. If they show underneath but not on top, a new panel has been put over the rusty original. Really the grot needs cutting out not covering up. This one is as it should be and shows no sign of repair or corrosion. The footwells are part of the structure so need to be in good condition. The driver's side being especially important as the brake pedal is attached to it as are the other pedals and to a lesser extent the steering box. A bare floor like this might be noisier and less refined but it dries easily. Old carpet or rubber mats trap water from leaks and contribute to corrosion.

suspension

RUSTY SPRINGS like this are normal as the inter leaf areas cannot retain paint. They will be slightly stiff for a few miles until they polish again and suggest the vehicle has been stood unused. If there was any bulging between the leaves then the rust is too severe and the ride will be horrible as there is no suspension they will also break easily off-road. These sit up well with plenty of clearance between the bump stops and axle top. In theory, if you lubricate springs they break more readily as the inter leaf friction is reduced. In practice, I would brush diesel on these or spray with WD40 and then paint the outside with grease. These will give quite a harsh ride as they are intended for an internal payload of about 750kgs. Replacements are not expensive at less than £200 for the vehicle. You can also fit Station Wagon springs to vehicles like this and, being dual rate, they give a better ride, or fit parabolic ones.

tyres

THE RADIALS are the correct size for the vehicle and will be the proper load rating. It is good practice to have them all the same make as well, but not essential. Don't mix crossplies and radials on the same vehicle, but if you have to, put the radials on the rear. These radial tyres will make the steering slightly heavier than the crossplies it was originally fitted with but the benefits of reduced noise, fuel costs and better handling make it well worth it. The wheels look good but they, too, will make the steering even heavier as they

have too much offset. As we are all used to power steering, a 109 in proper order will feel heavy so avoid exacerbating the problem. Standard wheels are cheap to buy so, again, don't turn the vehicle down for this. Heavy steering may also be a seized relay in the chassis or too much preload in the swivels so don't blame the wheels until these have been checked.

Back

THE INTERIOR of this ex-military Series III suggests little hard use as the aluminium is undamaged and the body sides still straight. There are no unintended holes in the floor either from corrosion or from a previous life as, say, a breakdown truck. Take a good look underneath the floor because the body crossmembers are steel and love to corrode with the aluminium they are next to. They can be easily replaced as they are only fitted with a couple of rivets at each end, but the floor itself is difficult to repair as the aluminium alloy strengthening ribs are spot welded to the floor panel. The spare wheel would be better in a proper bracket but will probably not fit as it is not an original wheel. Make certain your insurance company knows just how many seats there are in your vehicle. The one here needs a proper cushion to be used so would be best repaired or removed as appropriate to intended use. Equivalent condition 109s are cheaper than 88 inch wheelbases and the extra space in the rear and better driving seat adjustment range make them a good proposition.

Engine

THE ENGINE in this ex-military vehicle is light green, which is the colour of military rebuilds. It is also a Series II engine as the filler cap is not of the sealed breather type. It ought to be a five main bearing engine, but is probably a three. No need to worry as long as it is good, as many military vehicles end up with bits from varying years as items are replaced in service. Look for oil leaks and suspect a recently steam cleaned engine. I prefer a bit of honest dirt. Listen for knocks and harsh rumbles from the bottom end and watch for smoke on the over run from the exhaust. These engines often puff a little smoke when starting and is not a real cause for concern, but smoke on the overrun is a sign of wear in the valve gear. Take the oil filler cap off when running and look for fumes being pushed out. A good engine does not 'breathe' from the oil filler.

Seats

WHILE THEY look good, they may not be. Original seats have foams of varying high densities and are actually quite comfortable. New genuine Land Rover ones are as well. Some replacement ones are good but the cheaper ones have soft foam and it crushes easily so you sit on the wooden backing panel. It's not comfortable, especially on long journeys. So press down on the seat with a flat hand, and if you touch the base board, buy some better ones. Retro fitting car seats is a common thing on vehicles like this but with varying levels of success, improved seating is available from suppliers such as Exmoor trim and is well worth the investment.

It is a lot easier and cheaper to replace seats than chassis or mechanical bits, so do not pay any attention to them if they are poor. Their visibility is a good lever for price negotiation.

Chassis

THE CHASSIS looks solid, but there are signs of replacement outriggers being welded on from the vertical welds a few inches outboard of the outriggers. They have been done properly but check the new bit for corrosion as it can rot easily especially if not rust inhibited on the inside. Most chassis corrosion is from the inside as water and condensation collect in the lowest parts. Patch repairs are fine if welded continuously and use the original thickness of steel. Give the chassis a tap all over with a spanner. Good material has a ringing sound. Suspect areas will give a dull thud. Check all the electrical functions at the rear work, as welding repairs like this on the right hand chassis rail can melt the wiring as it is threaded down the right chassis internally. I always check the chassis on a road test. If you let the clutch out sharply and watch the join between the rear of the passenger door and the back body a good chassis will stay in the same position but a weak chassis will flex and allow the door to rise up as much as 10-15mm. If you can see movement, inspect the chassis closely.

This is an original Series III 109 chassis as it has pressed sidemembers and a seam weld along the top and bottom.

Rear crossmember

ONE OF the favourite rust points on the chassis is the rear cross member. They are not expensive to buy but are an involved job to replace properly. Some vehicles have two or three in their life but this one looks to be original as it has the old style rubber trailer plug hole on the right hand side and small holes in line with the main chassis rails. It is a good sign that the vehicle has not been worked hard but needs a good inspection and tapping with a spanner to check its integrity. On a replacement, the welding at the point of attachment needs checking, especially if towing is envisaged.

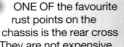

Top Tips
Purchasing knowledge in a nutshell...

1. A good secondhand vehicle should start from cold. Try and view the vehicle before it's been run that day to see how it starts.
2. Leave the engine running while inspecting the rest of the vehicle, this way you can see if it overheats.
3. If the vehicle is parked up against a wall or another vehicle it may mean that the owner is trying to hide panel damage.
4. Take a friend with you if you are going to pay in cash.
5. Check that the tyres aren't worn as a new set is expensive. Check the spare too.

WHAT ELSE CAN I GET FOR *£2,500?*

Range Rover

A LATE eighties Range Rover V8 is easily bought for this price, the only factory diesel worth having is the usually more expensive Tdi. Avoid conversions as they are problematic. A Tdi conversion with a factory kit is fine though. You will get a good late eighties vehicle for this or even an early nineties one with low spec.

As with any vehicle at this price buy the condition, not the age, and don't dismiss older vehicles – a good early eighties vehicle is worth this much if in sound genuine condition. The Classic Range Rover has an enthusiastic following and once all the grot has been scrapped, remaining good vehicles will hold and ultimately rise in value – even more so if you can find something a little different which will be an investment.

Look for corrosion in the floor, wheel arches, sills, the footwells and inner wings. All body corrosion is repairable if the price justifies it, but it is better to buy a sound vehicle in the first place. The exterior panels also corrode but can be replaced.

Doors, bonnet and both tailgates corrode. The engines are usually good but can suffer head gasket failure. The Efi system on the 3.5 isn't as reliable as the type used on the 3.9 but that's not a reason not to buy one.

Discovery

WHATEVER YOU do in this price range buy the condition and not the age. One ought to be able to buy quite a good H/J reg 1991 for this sort of money that has not had commercial use, is tidy inside and will have a useful residual life. If you don't do lots of miles don't dismiss a V8 or Mpi petrol one as you will get a much later vehicle for the money. The Mpi never really found favour with the buying public and does not fetch a lot secondhand. It is reasonable to find quite late ones for this money even as recent as L/M reg. The most valuable are the Tdi diesels as the engine alone is worth £1,000.

While sunroofs and roof rails are good, if they aren't fitted, they don't leak. The rear alpine lights are fitted to all of them and do leak. Lift the carpet in the back and look at the state of the floor. They corrode readily as does the rear body crossmember under the door. The sills corrode both under the carpets and the bits you can see underneath. The wheel arches corrode at the rear and the footwells as well. Under the bonnet the inner wings are also rust. All the rusty bits are repairable but it is much better to buy a good one.

Once you have found one that is not too rusty check the gearbox for clunks suggesting main shaft wear. The synchromesh will be a bit weak but it is par for the course at this sort of price. A Tdi engine is usually fine but check if it has had a cambelt recently and look for signs of overheating or water loss as they are prone to head gasket failure or even cracked heads.

90s and 110s

DEFENDERS HAVE always been the best financial performers of all Land Rover products and at a given age will retain a greater percentage of the original purchase cost. Consequently, even though a Discovery cost a lot more when new, now you will get an older Defender for the same money. The more expensive when new Defenders such as the Station Wagon 110 or the 130 will always have that extra value so this money will buy a 90 van from the early nineties with Tdi power. It will also buy a 110 van with a Tdi, but a genuine Station Wagon 90 and 110 will still be the old turbo engine which is best avoided in these heavy vehicles.

A V8 130 probably ex-utility company is on the cards for this level of cash. It is best to spend a bit more on a Station Wagon with the Tdi engine though a high mileage one with a Tdi only fetched £2,400 at Brightwell's auction a few weeks ago. If this is the limit of your funds look for an older V8 possibly running on LPG. It is unrealistic to expect a Defender in immaculate condition for this money.

Have a good hard look at the chassis especially the rear end and the outriggers for latent corrosion or sub standard repairs. Check the bulkhead in the footwells and outer top corners. Look for corrosion in the rear floor. Check the gearbox for clunks and noise, ask about cam belt history.

FIND OUT MORE

THERE ARE a number of different outlets available from where you can purchase secondhand Land Rovers.

- ■ AUCTIONS
- ■ INTERNET AUCTIONS
- ■ CLASSIFIEDS
- ■ FRANCHISED DEALERS
- ■ INDEPENDENT DEALERS

IN THE MARKET PLACE

■ **1989 Range Rover 3.5 Vogue SE 4dr Auto Station Wagon,** 94,000 miles. Leather and loads of toys. £2,250

1995 Land Rover Discovery 300 Tdi 3 door, manual, Station Wagon, diesel, 168,000 miles, red. £2,250

1992 Land Rover Discovery 200 Tdi 3 door, manual, Station Wagon, diesel, 130,000 miles, full service history. £2,295

1990 Range Rover 3.9 EFi Vogue 4dr Auto Estate, petrol, 123,000 miles, lots of extras. £2,299

1992 Land Rover Discovery Tdi, one lady owner from new, 150,000 miles. £2,300

1991 Land Rover Discovery V8, 5 door, Green. £2,350

1976 Land Rover Lightweight, 2.25 petrol (unleaded head), hard top with side windows, alpines and sunroof, tow bar. £2,450

1992 Land Rover Discovery Tdi 3 door, excellent for year, 140,000 miles, just been cambelted. £2,495

1988 Land Rover Defender 90 turbo diesel, 62,240 miles, Blue. £2,495

1953 Land Rover Series One Pick Up Hodges, green, Tax exempt. £2,500

1985 Land Rover Defender 90 diesel, 80,000 miles, bodywork and interior are immaculate. £2,500

1966 Land Rover Series II LWB, reconditioned engine, lots of new parts. £2,500

WHAT CAN I GET FOR £5,000?

There's masses of choice in this price range, so don't be tempted by the first thing you see – spread your net wide and shop around

MOST OF us buy a car based on what we can afford rather than setting out with a distinct vehicle in mind. So, with £5,000 carefully zipped up in an inside pocket, we set off to find the Lode Lane chariot that would press all the right buttons.

Immediately obvious at that price would be a 90, but we've already got a 200Tdi Soft Top on the **LRM** fleet, so another one didn't immediately appeal. Anyway, 90s at this price are rather 'workhorse-ish' and we'd hoped to root out something with a bit of pazzaz and a few more creature comforts.

A 110 would be nice and we could find some good examples, particularly hardtops at this price but, again, suitability for our purpose wasn't being met. We wanted a smart vehicle that would mainly be for on-road commuting, would be comfortable and would be spacious.

So, a Discovery made obvious sense. But it soon became apparent that we'd have to dip a bit deeper into the piggy bank for the couple of grand extra it would take find a tidy one with reasonable mileage.

Doesn't matter how much you've got to spend, you always need that little bit more. But we had our limit, so it was on to the next category.

Low priced Freelanders make an excellent purchase, but it will be an early example and could be susceptible to electronics and transmission problems. Not that a bit of potential repair work should rule out a purchase but, to be honest, older Freelanders aren't that exciting.

But Classic Range Rovers *are* exciting and, at £5,000, there are plenty of examples of some very fine machinery to be had. It's true what they say, you do get a lot of car for your money.

We finally plumped for this very low mileage 3.9 SE from our own classified ad pages. After a thorough going over it was pronounced clean and a sound purchase, and it now adorns the car park at **LRM** Towers.

It's in tip-top condition and proves that the Classic Range Rover is an absolute bargain.

J193 UDU

engine

THE PETROL engines fitted to these Range Rovers are the 3.5-litre and 3.9-litre V8s. Ours is a low mileage 3.9, but as long as they have had regular oil changes, 250,000 miles are not unusual. Make sure you check for 'weeping' from head gaskets, camshafts and followers.

The early diesel engines were the 2.4 and 2.5 VMs. They are solid engines, but look out for problems with cylinder heads and liners. Later on, Land Rover started to fit the 200 and 300Tdi engines. These are better engines but do have their own problems with the heads cracking and the timing belt going too many miles without change. It is suggested that if you have no proof of when the timing belt was last changed, get it done straight away.

A professional LPG conversion will ease running costs.

chassis plate

THE CHASSIS number is in roughly the same place on all Classic Range Rovers. It is situated between four steering box holding bolts on the outside of the right hand chassis leg. It moved forward slightly on the soft dash and air suspension models. It can also be found on an aluminium plate that is rivetted to the slam panel on the front bonnet. On the later vehicles you can see it through the windscreen on the dash.

choices

THE RANGE Rover Classic is a highly sought after Land Rover. The best example of which is arguably the 1995 'Soft Dash'. The 4.2-litre engine that's fitted to this model is probably the best-ever Rover V8. There is only a limited supply of these vehicles and they are in high demand. That's why examples in good condition still fetch a premium. The hardest of these vehicles to find are the 'Soft Dash' LSE (long wheelbase) and the Vogue 300Tdi Automatic.

Higher specification Range Rovers that you are likely to be interested in at this price have many electrical gadgets. These extras are, for many people, part of the appeal of these vehicles. However, they can, and do, go wrong. Electric windows and central locking should be checked. The electrics that are involved with the engine are usually pretty reliable. Make sure that there are no leaks in the power steering unit. They can be fixed for around £150 if there are problems.

Later models often have ABS and air suspension. These are both worth having but are tiresome or near impossible to fix yourself if they go wrong.

The older fuel tanks can corrode so look out for this. Newer ones fitted with plastic fuel tanks are better but the fuel pipes on the top of them can still corrode.

Interiors can be well worn and headlinings come away. These can be replaced at a reasonable cost and should be taken into consideration.

chassis

THERE ARE less problems with rotting on the Range Rovers than Series vehicles of similar ages but there are a few areas that are worth inspecting. Take a look at the ends of the body mounts and by the fuel tank at the rear of the vehicle. There are two steel fuel pipes running down the right hand side of an Efi chassis. They often corrode and then leak. If they are pitted they will need immediate replacement.

transmission

THE FIRST Range Rovers had a clunky four speed gear box, but this is unlikely to be found on a model in this price range. The long and short stick five speeds do have problems with the bearings and synchromesh. It is quite common for these old Range Rovers to clunk when taking up drive and changing gear. This will be because the back end of the mainshaft is badly worn. It is advisable to

avoid such vehicles as this problem is time consuming and expensive to repair. At the very least, get this taken into consideration in the asking price. The automatic gearboxes are mainly very good, they will either be working well or broken.

body

THE RANGE Rover's body is prone to rotting. The footwells and front inner wings should be checked. The sills and bottoms of A and B posts. On the four door Range Rovers inspect the base of the C post where the rear door shuts, and the seat belt mountings. At the rear of the vehicle the body cross member and the inner wings rot. Tailgates, all the doors and newer models bonnets all rot.

Spares can be bought for all these parts but they can cost. They can also be costly to fit.

Air conditioning on the older vehicles can be expensive to fix as they don't run on the new refrigerant, there is no problem with later vehicles.

WHAT ELSE CAN I GET FOR £5,000?

90 and 110

THE 90s and 110s available at this price are likely to be well used hard tops with high mileage. However, if you shop around you can find yourself a good deal.

● The main thing to look out for when purchasing one of these vehicles is corrosion. It may not be immediately apparent if the vehicle has started to corrode, so be extra vigilant. The main corrosion areas are chassis outriggers and rear cross members.
● A 90 that has been used outdoors on a farm for years is far more likely to be corroded than one that has been kept in a garage.
● The rubber timing belt on the diesel engined examples (apart from the 2.25) needs to be regularly replaced, so ask for a history.
● The petrol engines should be fine. There is often a problem with rust on the bulkheads so take a look.
● The rear door may crack or corrode especially if the spare wheel is attached.
● Finally, suspension bushes can wear badly, axles and steering boxes also can leak.

FREELANDER

IF YOU shop around it is now possible to pick up a Freelander at this price. They will be the earlier models, usually with high mileage. It is also likely that they will be of a low specification, an unpopular colour (white, for example) or both.

These early Freelanders were fitted with Rover car engines and are, on the whole, sound, reliable motors. The transmissions are very good, just be cautious of noisy rear differentials on high mileage vehicles.

The monocoque chassis doesn't rust. Check all the electronics work and the sunroof opens properly. Window lift cables break so check that they work.

A warning about the Freelander's ABS and Hill Descent Control: they can stop working. However, most Freelanders available for this price won't have Hill Descent Control or air conditioning.

Top Tips

Purchasing knowledge in a nutshell...

- Make sure you check the tread on all tyres, including the spare. Tyres can be very expensive to replace.

- Don't be overly enthusiastic about a vehicle. If the dealer picks up on this he may hold out for a higher price than you could otherwise achieve.

- Read the service history. Make sure there is nothing suspicious.

- Don't buy a vehicle in the rain. The paint work on a wet car always looks good.

- Don't buy a vehicle at night. You may miss a number of problems that will become apparent in the daylight.

DISCOVERY

YOU SHOULD be able to find a reasonable example of a Discovery Series One for this price. Although they are extremely capable off-road vehicles, many were bought as family cars due to their ability to seat up to seven people – these are usually in a better condition.

The engines are generally good but there are a few niggles with head problems and cambelt failure so it's worth checking these out. Inner wings, footwells, sills and rear body cross members often rot especially in older vehicles.

Body seams and sunroofs may leak, causing the rear floor to corrode. The chassis doesn't rot and neither does the plastic fuel tank. The Discovery has a high centre of gravity so look out for worn suspension bushes effecting the handling.

Rear bumpers can corrode. On top of the plastic fuel tank, the fuel pipes can rot. This can either let air into the fuel system or water into the tank. Finally test all the electronics to make sure they work properly.

FIND OUT MORE

THERE ARE a number of different outlets available from where you can purchase secondhand Land Rovers. Try these more common ones.

AUCTIONS If you know what to look out for, an auction can be a great way to pick up a bargain Land Rover. Brightwells holds a specialist 4x4 auction. To find out more visit *www.brightwells.com* or phone 01568 611325.

INTERNET AUCTIONS These days you can buy a new Land Rover without leaving the comfort of your own home via an internet auction site. The most popular of these being *www.ebay.com*.

CLASSIFIEDS Many vehicles are available within *LRM* Classifieds, with hundreds of vehicles for sale each month.

FRANCHISED DEALERS For further information about Land Rover dealerships and the service they offer, visit their website *www.landrover.com*.

INDEPENDENT DEALERS For information on Land Rovers for sale, you can trawl the *LRM* ads.

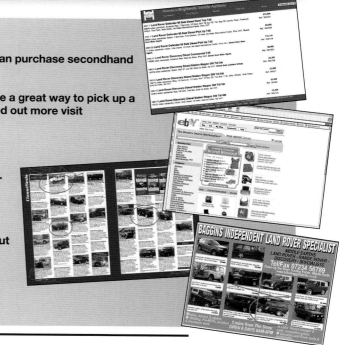

WHAT CAN I GET FOR £8,000?

DISCOVERY
300Tdi GS
Built in 1997
Cost £7,995 at a
local independent
4x4 specialist

FOR:
Unworn seats
Wood effect dash
Clean 300
Tdi engine

AGAINST:
Rusty inner wing
corroding chassis

THERE'S PLENTY of choice in this price bracket and a good, solid example of a first generation Discovery caught our eye at an independent Land Rover dealership. Close inspection did reveal a few potential problems that will need sorting out before too long.

The vehicle looks good in this popular colour. Tyres are fine and all panels line up well, suggesting no accident repairs. The paintwork is good and headlights are untarnished, though are cheap to replace if they are.

Externally it looks tidy and to be a good buy, but any potential buyer should be aware that there is already quite a lot of corrosion biting into the structure. If it were a ten or 12-year-old vehicle then that is par for the course, you would struggle to find an ageing Discovery without any corrosion or rusting but is slightly disheartening to find it on one of this age. However, the vehicle originates from Scotland and this could explain the apparent early corrosion. At £8,000, it is worth remembering that other options are available to you, shop around before you buy.

OUR CHOICE

boot corner

THIS IS a common corrosion point with the join of the steel frame and alloy skin. This one has creeping corrosion under the paint and will eventually blister with white powder underneath. While the scabs are not too bad it has been painted before as the 'Tdi' badge has been masked round rather than removed and renewed. It is a little disappointing to see it returning.

driver's seat

THE EDGES of the seats tend to wear where the driver rubs across it when getting in and out. This one is really good, suggesting that the vehicle has not done much work or has had a new seatbase. Leather is much more hard wearing than cloth but much more expensive to sort out when it is worn.

inside door

THIS PART of the structure looks to be good, though the doors themselves corrode due to having a steel frame and an alloy skin. Check along the bottom edge for corrosion or repairs.

wheels

THE WHEELS look good and the paintwork is fine. The edges are prone to parking rash, but these look in good condition. It has a good set of Michelin tyres with lots of tread and no signs of scrubbing, suggesting the previous owner has spent on good quality items for the vehicle. Cheap remoulds, though legal, might suggest penny pinching in other areas as well.

dash

THE DASH looks to be tidy and the wood effect looks good in the vehicle. It may not be a factory original, but a retrofitted upgrade. Be wary of base model vehicles being passed off as higher spec more expensive models. If air conditioning is fitted, check it works as it can be expensive to repair, though re-gassing is cheap.

Check the spec expected on the model in question and look on the V5 – it usually tells you the model type. Do not rely on

the sticker on the wing

The dash is prone to lifting on the nearside next to the window due to a manufacturing defect. Many have been replaced under warranty or a special plate bolted through it to hold it down, but it should not be bulging upwards.

inside rust

THIS RUST on the inner wing is quite advanced and it will only be a matter of time before the vehicle fails the MOT. It is quite disappointing to see it on only a seven-year-old vehicle, but it is quite common. Scraping it off

and treating it with a rust converter might delay replacement inner wings for a while – you will find it difficult to find a Discovery without corrosion at all.

engine

THE 300Tdi looks to be clean, but not cleaned recently which is the best sort to see as the light dirt looks to be from recent usage. A fresh steam clean might be concealing oil leaks. All the clips on the pipes look to be in place and all electrical fixings look to be as it left the factory, which suggests it has not been much trouble to anyone.

This engine has a tendency for timing belt trouble so needs replacing unless it has been done recently with the latest modified bits. Don't accept someone's word it has been done ask, to see the invoice.

inside bonnet

THE FRONT panel is also quite corroded with it well established. A lot of the high up in the body corrosion is from salt water spray on winter roads. Converted and stabilised it will last a few years but, again, it is slightly disappointing to see it.

transmission

THE R380 gearbox is prone to syncromesh problems, especially getting into lower gears when cold. The rear mainshaft can also be a problem, though the revised gears used on later vehicles are not so troublesome as on older ones. The main gear knob is a good indication that the mileage covered is accurate. They go smooth by about 75,000 miles and the gear positions are unreadable at 100,000.

chassis

THERE IS no evidence of damage from off-road use. The bottom of the chassis and the crossmembers are straight and true with no bashes from rocks. There are no bulges or welding repairs from accident damage, so it looks a genuine vehicle.

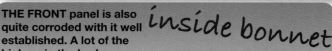

LAND ROVER

R975 DNS
INVERCLYDE GREENOCK

1. Check the driver's seat and carpet for signs of wear, especially if the mileage is low.
2. Focus on a reflection in the paint work, a hazy reflection can indicate a filler has been used.
3. Check the chassis number on the vehicle and the registration document is the same.
4. If possible take an unbiased mechanic along with you for advice.
5. The engine shouldn't be overly noisey or smokey, even on old vehicles.

back arch

THE REAR arch corrodes as road debris sits on it and stays damp. It is also prone to cracking where there is a bolt through it into the mudflap supporting panel. This one looks to be fine and unmarked.

VIN plate

THE VIN plate looks to be un-tampered with and should be the same as the one in the windscreen and on the chassis on the right hand side between the four bolts that hold the steering box on to the chassis. They all need to match the V5c document and MOT.

boot corner

THIS IS a favourite rust point on a Discovery and the corrosion starts on the under edge and creeps up. This example should be treated with a rust killer and repainted, preferably with a stone chip resistant material underneath. Though not too nice to see, it is good that it hasn't been hidden with a quick bodge.

extra seats

THE SEVEN seat version of Discoverys is always more popular. The seats are fine for adults, but are not as good as the Series II or III. If you do not need them, don't pay the extra few hundred pounds that seven-seat vehicles fetch. If not fitted, all the mounting points are in the shell. Secondhand ones can be bought easily if you find an otherwise good five-seat.

The rear load bay does not appear to have had commercial use as the floor covering looks tidy and there is not much bashing and bruising on the seatbacks.

chassis

THERE IS quite a lot of scale and corrosion on the outside of the chassis. Discoverys are not prone to chassis corrosion, but this one is starting to rust. If cleaned off and treated it will last quite a long time, but if left alone it will only be a couple of years before the chassis needs welding repairs. The axles rust as well with pitting of the case often leading to oil leaks. Some even need new axles or a new diff pan welding on.

panels

THE PANELS that go down from the floor and support the top of the mud flaps and the bottom of the outer wing are in the firing line for all the stones and muck thrown up by the wheels. They corrode readily as they are a thin steel sheet. They are bolted on and easy to replace, and quite inexpensive. This one seems to have had new ones fitted. For added protection, it could also do with the mud flaps, as they stop the rear window getting dirty so quickly.

inner wheel arch

THE BOX section under the door is prone to corrosion and is replaceable, as is the rear bumper itself. The biggest problem is the boot floor. It needs the rear plastic strip unscrewing to allow the carpet to be lifted and inspected underneath.

Even vehicles of this age can have penetrating corrosion in the floor. It can be inspected from underneath if the vendor will not allow the carpet to be lifted, but is hard to see properly as the fuel tank is in the way. There are other visible corrosion warning signs on this vehicle, so the sills and rear floor and front footwells need a careful inspection under the carpets.

IN THE MARKET PLACE

Defender Stationwagon

YOU WILL get an N, P or R Station Wagon for this sort of money and they will keep more of your money for longer than any other Land Rover product. The 110 can carry up to 12 people, though it is not ideal. It is good for up to nine.

The Tdi engines have the same problems as discussed for the Discovery, as does the gearbox. Chassis-wise, the back ends suffer first and the bulkhead is prone to rust. The doors are also prone to corrosion of the inner framing but replacements are not expensive or difficult to fit. There is no automatic option and you will not buy one of the limited editions that were built as an auto for this little yet. The spotwelds and exposed rivets are factory fitted and not a sign of damage repairs.

Commercial use is quite common and many on offer might have a public utility as first owner. The 12-seat is classed as a minibus and the VAT is reclaimable by business owners. Be careful when buying at auction as it can be added to the hammer price. Most sought after is the Metallic Red ten-seat 110.

Freelander

THE PETROL engines can be troublesome but revised head gaskets cure the problems. The Td4 diesel is excellent and with the steptronic gearbox option makes you wonder why anyone buys a manual.

Corrosion is not really an issue, as they seem to be well protected and much plastic is used in the bumpers and front wings. Rear diffs hum but do not fail until very noisy. The bearings on the propshaft either side of the viscous coupling give trouble as does the VCU itself. Though expensive, they are easy to change.

The driver's door drop glass cables break but are not difficult and only cost £100 in bits. The other doors are less prone as they get used less. The Hill Descent Control is formidable off-road but may not work. On manuals, it is often a broken wire in the gear lever.

Don't underestimate the off-road performance as they will do everything as well as or better than any other Land Rover product. They will only tow two tons, which includes most caravans but not big transport trailers.

P38A Range Rover

YOU CAN buy quite a nice one for this money, though the petrol ones are thirsty and suffer engine problems. Body corrosion is not a problem as they are well protected and it is only the rear tailgate that is a weak point.

A mid-nineties P or R reg diesel is quite a good vehicle to run and easily found for £8,000. The automatic is reliable and good even with the diesel but it does drop the performance and they do not take kindly to big trailers. They are really good off-road and a relaxed cruiser on the motorway, so all uses are excelled at.

While corrosion is not the nemesis of a P38a owner, the electrical system is, with problems in all the electronic controlled systems. Body, air suspension, engine, gearbox, heating and cooling all have computers and they do go wrong. Check all the functions, as problems such as the heater blowing hot air when you want cold, or visa versa, are difficult to spot and expensive to sort out.

The driving experience is excellent and, though not thought of as highly as the old Classic or the third generation Range Rover, they still offer good value at this sort of age. The depreciation has slowed down a bit but they are still dropping.

Most sought after blue or grey diesel automatic HSE.

FIND OUT MORE

■ AUCTIONS - Knowledgeable buyers can pick up a real bargain, but can be risky for first time buyers.

■ INTERNET AUCTIONS - Pick from a whole range of vehicles without leaving your desk but nothing is certain in this new market place.

■ CLASSIFIEDS - LRM has the biggest selection around, see the green pages each month.

■ FRANCHISED DEALERS - Catering for the top end of the market they tend to be be more expensive but quality is guaranteed.

■ INDEPENDENT DEALERS - Helpful staff will assist you in making the right purchase, with many now offering finance deals.

WHAT CAN I GET FOR

£12,000?

1999 DEFENDER 110 CSW

On sale at RJ Land Rovers
£12,000 + VAT

FOR:
Tidy bodywork
Not used off-road
No corrosion evident
Genuine mileage

AGAINST:
Top of its price range
Minor blemishes
Price subject to VAT
(which would be a plus point
for a VAT-registered purchaser)

THERE'S REALLY nothing to beat a Defender 110 Station Wagon. Its load and people carrying ability is outstanding, its longevity is legendary and it's every bit a Land Rover.

We were looking for a vehicle with all-round capability and nothing, not even a Discovery, tops the 110 CSW. We found this excellent example at RJ Land Rovers in Cambridgeshire.

The colour looks good on this model and complements the silver of the alloy wheels. It is metallic with a clear coat on top and looks to be mostly, if not totally, original factory finish.

The vehicle also stands well and is square. It looks to have been used as a 'car' rather than an off-roader, so is really tidy for its age.

The level of wear on the seats, steering wheel, gear lever and the vehicle's general appearance would suggest the odometer reading of 77,000 miles is correct. There is no corrosion evident on the front bulkhead or signs of repair.

It is only a relatively young Defender, but rust can be found on others this age. It needs a thorough wax injection in all the cavities and underneath, the timing belt history investigating or replacing and a bit of paint-work attending to.

As it is at the top of the price range for this sort of year we would try to get these items included in the price, or get a bit off.

chequerplate

CHEQUER PLATE is often applied to vehicles to disguise damage rather than to provide an anti-slip surface or protect the body-work. It is also often used to enhance appearance. Though not to everyone's taste it has been fitted for looks in this case as the wings look perfect other-wise. There is no distortion, the seams are all perfect and undisturbed, just as they ought to be. Removing it leaves holes, so once on it is there forever.

bumper

THE CHASSIS looks straight and has not suffered any impact damage. There is a slight trace of rust here that would benefit from treating and waxing. The VIN number is stamped on the chassis on the outside of the bracket that runs under the bumper forward of the lashing eye fixing bolt, though is on the other side of the vehicle on the right hand chassis leg.

chassis

THE CHASSIS is tidy and not corroded. There is no damage from off-roading. It has been waxed at some point in the past and has a nice honest build up of dust and debris. It would pay to re-wax it for long term protection, especially internally. The axles look good and there is no damage to front diff housing, further suggesting little off road use.

dash

THE INTERIOR looks good and the top of the dash is tidy. There has, in the past, been an item of equipment screwed to the under dash such as a CD player or other type of radio. It has left some unsightly holes that might be improved with a couple of plastic trim plugs and slightly spoils the rest of the interior. The other trim just needs to be pushed back in place.

door

THE DOOR frames look OK and there is no corrosion. The station wagons are prone to corrosion of the box section in the body that forms the angled part of the rear door frame. The doors themselves are prone to corrosion of the steel frame, though it is readily visible when they are open. This vehicle seems to be corrosion free and would also respond to a thorough waxing of the body frame and door frames.

hinge

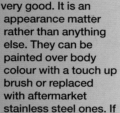

THE PLATING on the hinge screws at this age was not very good. It is an appearance matter rather than anything else. They can be painted over body colour with a touch up brush or replaced with aftermarket stainless steel ones. If you intend to keep it for a long time this is the best option as they last forever. It is easy to do – if you do one at a time you do not lose the setting. Whilst they are out it is an ideal place to get access into the inside of the bulkhead and spray in lots of cavity protection wax as prevention of corrosion is easier than cure.

engine

IT IS nice to see honest dirt on this 300Tdi engine. It is in a used condition but seems to be dry and tidy – not recently cleaned which might have hidden oil leaks. All the clips, nuts and bolts look to be untouched. It should have had a timing belt replacement recently and if the invoice for the job or service book stamp is not available it needs replacing now. The Td5 diesel has a chain driven camshaft so all those timing belt problems that have afflicted Land Rover diesels since 1983 were wiped out at the stroke of a pencil in 1998 when that engine came out.

scratch

WHILST IT is a bit disappointing to see, it is probably a bigger job to sort out than is justified. It can be improved a little bit by careful use of a touch up brush or repainted completely.

corrosion

THIS CORROSION is a bit more disappointing to see but can be sanded out and resprayed. It will not improve with time so would be best resprayed now, especially as the front eyebrow would look better painted at the same time. I would estimate about £200-£250 to have both of these sprayed professionally. It stems from the electrolytic action of two dissimilar metals (steel chassis, aluminum body) reacting with salt water from the road as an electrolyte. The bracket needs bending forward slightly and painting behind as well. If we were intending to keep the vehicle for a long time, we would cut a polythene or thin rubber gasket to fit between to keep them separate and slop a load of grease in the joint as we tightened it up after painting between them as well. We would do the same with the other body mounts as well, then wax it thoroughly from behind.

wheels

THE ALLOYS are prone to damage especially if run along the kerb. They also suffer from corrosion and separation of the paint and lacquer from the base. These wheels look fine.

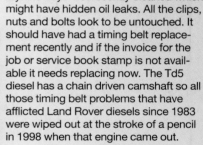

rear door and spare

THE PLASTIC trim is slightly damaged on the rear door. It probably rubs on the check strap and would look better or even unnoticeable if trimmed off with a sharp knife.

Tyre is new and unused. It is also is the same make as the others on the vehicle and they look in good condition as well, with plenty of life remaining. They are a good make and not remoulds, all positive factors for the vehicle.

back door

HAS NOT had a hard commercial life as sill section is not damaged or scratched. The carpet looks to be original and in good condition. The door itself appears sound, although may have fatigue cracking on spare wheel mount.

step

THE STEP has been rubbed down something, such as a high kerb, and has cut through the rubber. It is a common problem if the steps are left in the down position. They seize up easily so need regular lubrication to the hinges if to be kept in working order.

seats

THE FRONT seats are tidy especially where they tend to wear on the outer edge where you slide over them when entering the vehicle. The seatbelts are prone to damage as they get a bit tired and do not retract quickly, getting trapped in the door lock as the door is shut, but these are perfect.

rear crossmember

LOOKS TO be straight and true. The rear step is spring loaded and not usually in the down position, if left it will be damaged if you tow a trailer. The tow hitch does not seem to have had much use, if any at all, as the paint is still unworn on it. Towing puts more stress on a vehicle, so the less it has done the better. 110s suffer chassis corrosion, especially at the back, and it needs careful examination, but this one looks fine.

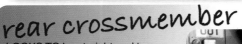

arch

THERE IS no corrosion or damage to the rear arch and the seatbelt mounting points look to be fine. They are prone to rusting as they suffer all the stones and mud thrown up by the back wheels. The general condition would suggest it has not had a lot of use in winter salt.

VAT

AS A 12 seat vehicle in the UK this Land Rover is classed as a minibus and as a commercial vehicle. The first and subsequent owners would be able to reclaim the VAT if they were registered for VAT and later on, when sold off, would charge it on its disposal price just as if it were a van or pick up Land Rover.

This situation does not apply to nine or ten seat 110s as built, or to six or seven seat 90s as they are classed as cars and sold with VAT included as new – only when sold on by a dealer is further VAT paid as a proportion of their profit margin.

If a dealer buys a commercial vehicle such as this 110 from a company that is VAT registered he will advertise it as £X + VAT, but if he buys from a private individual who has not reclaimed the VAT, he can treat it as he would a 'car' and only pay VAT on his mark up.

A vehicle that's not '+ VAT' suggests the last owner was a private individual which is a good sign that it hasn't had heavy commercial use.

Top Tips

Purchasing knowledge in a nutshell...

1. Get your car checked by the HPI, RAC or AA. They can tell you if the car has money owing on it, if it's been written off, or if it's stolen.

2. Check to see if the car has been resprayed, this is a good indication the car has been involved in an accident. All the panel colours should match exactly.

3. Look at the window rubbers for signs of overspray.

4. If you show your cash late on in a deal it can help you secure a low price.

5. Remember to haggle – you can always raise your offer.

VIN plate

PLATE LOOKS original and untampered with. Check the number is same as on chassis, windscreen and on all the paperwork. On older vehicles it is wise to check it has always been a station wagon and is not a built up vehicle on a van chassis. Land Rover Traceability will confirm the build details of more recent vehicles and BMIHT at Gaydon those of older vehicles. There is no evidence to suggest this vehicle is anything other than a factory built one. Look for bits with different colours of paint showing and items of a different age to that which the vehicle is supposed to be. There is no problem with rebuilds as long as the price reflects it.

WHAT ELSE CAN I GET FOR £12,000?

> £12000

IN THE MARKET PLACE

1997 Defender 90 Station Wagon. 300 Tdi. Monte Carlo blue. Alloy wheels. Tow pack. Moorland cloth upholstery. 22,000 miles. **£11,995**

2000 Discovery Td5. 5-speed manual. Traction control. Alloy wheels. Light guards front and rear. A-bar. Running boards. 49,000 miles. **£11,995**

1998 Defender 90 County Station Wagon Tdi. Blue. 70,000 Miles. Alloy wheels. Sunroof. Power steering. A bar with spotlamps. Side and rear steps. Towpack. Lamp Guards. Front and Rear Mudflaps. Cloth interior. **£11,995**

2003 Freelander Kalahari Td4. Monte Carlo blue. 23,000 miles. Black leather/Alacantara trim. Air-con. 6 disk CD. 17" alloys. Roofrails and bars. **£11,750**

2003 Freelander Td4 Serengeti. 5 Doors. Manual. 32,638 miles. Black. Adjustable lumbar support. Adjustable steering column. Air con. Alloy wheels. Immobiliser. Power socket. Tinted glass. **£11,795**

1998 Range Rover DSE. 61000 miles. Automatic. Blue with piped light stone leather. Climate control. Harmon Kardon six disc CD. Remote locking. Detachable tow bar. Cruise control. Multi function steering wheel. **£11,950**

2000 Discovery 2.5 Td5 XS. 7 seat. Manual. 89,110 miles. Metallic Oslo blue. Adjustable steering column/wheel. Alloy wheels. Half leather upholstery. **£11,995**

P38A Range Rover

THIS IS a lot of car for the money, however with all the computers and electronics fitted there can be big lists of problems on older vehicles. By older we don't mean 20 or 30 years, we mean six or seven years old. The 2000 model year onwards vehicles are more reliable and you ought to be able to buy a good one for this money – 1999-2000 V/W reg 72,000 miles.

The later clear lights make them look more recent, though many older vehicles have had them retrofitted. There is not really a base model, so all have air suspension, the higher spec ones have leather seats and climate control.

Corrosion is not a big issue, although the lower rear tailgate can cause problems. The BMW 2.5-litre engine is reliable, as is the auto gearbox. The manual is the same R380 as used in the Defender and Discovery, therefore gives similar problems. Most problems with the vehicles are of an electronic or electrical nature. They commonly include suspension problems, locking, heating and air conditioning – even lighting problems.

Discovery Series II

FOR THE budget you can buy a five year old Discovery Td5 ES – W reg 60,000 miles – with all the bells and whistles, or an even newer one with a lower standard of extras. There are not as many problems with the Series II Discovery as there are with the older one and corrosion of the bodyshell in particular is not so rampant. As with the Defender, the engine is quite reliable, though can be prone to head gasket problems. If the fuel filter is changed at proper service intervals or when the water warning light comes on, the fuel system gives little trouble. The manual gearboxes can be a bit clunky with higher miles, especially on second gear. Unlike the Defender Td5 the Discovery has an automatic gearbox option.

It is more sought after than the manual, and similar vehicles are worth about £1000 more if automatic. The seven seat option also adds about £500 to the value. The ACE cornering system works well and makes the driving more car-like, as there is a lot less body roll. Trailer work can confuse it, although it usually resets itself. The self levelling air suspension on the rear end is also a good item on the higher spec vehicles but can give trouble with perished air bags.

Freelander

DIESEL STATION wagons are dropping in price quickly, now the dealers are giving big discounts on new vehicles in the run up to the new model launch. A three year old one – 2002 52 plate 25-30,000 miles – with a reasonable spec can be found for this money. They do not have many problems and seem to be almost corrosion free, even the oldest 1997 ones do not seem to have rusted much. The main problems seem to be the rear differentials and centre viscous coupling. At the sort

of age and mileage you can buy for £12,000 they ought not to be much of a problem. It would pay to buy one that is still within the manufacturer's three year warranty, if you can find one, as even if it is only a few weeks remaining any problems can be fixed for free.

The automatic 'Steptronic' gearbox seems to be vice free but adds to the value so an automatic will be slightly older. The BMW Td4 diesel is economical and very reliable and it is almost petrol like in regards to performance and lack of noise. Check all the extras such as the air con and hill descent work properly.

FIND OUT MORE

■ **AUCTIONS** - Knowledgeable buyers can pick up a real bargain, but can be risky for first time buyers. Set yourself a firm budget and stick to it.

■ **INTERNET AUCTIONS** - Pick from a whole range of vehicles without leaving your desk but nothing is certain in this new market place.

■ **CLASSIFIEDS** - **LRM** has the biggest selection around, see the Green Pages every month.

■ **FRANCHISED DEALERS** - Catering for the top end of the market they tend to be be more expensive but quality is guaranteed.

■ **INDEPENDENT DEALERS** - Helpful staff will assist you in making the right purchase, with many now offering finance deals.

A Series One 88 inch model combines all that's best in the early model Land Rover

THE SERIES One 88 is an ideal vehicle to own, especially if you want to combine the look of these vehicles with the best driving standard possible. These vehicles also respond well to a limited amount of upgrading without compromising the looks or usability or even the originality as many upgrades can be reversed.

Later engines are a common fitment, especially for the original diesel engine as it is considered underpowered by today's standards. Spare parts have been a problem for the 2-litre diesels for some years, so many have been replaced with the later 2,286cc engines either diesel or petrol. While it is harder to fit this engine in vehicles that were built as petrol powered, both types of 2,286cc engine can be fitted with a simple gearbox bellhousing swap as well.

Overdrives are another common addition and modern radial tyres improve the handling remarkably, though they make the steering a little heavier as well. The brakes can be upgraded with a servo, and the bigger set up from a long wheelbase model and modern parabolic springs are a firm favourite as they give a great improvement over worn out originals. New original specification springs also work wonders as well.

problem solving

Many current owners want to enjoy the pleasure of soft top motoring. In previous lives though, many were converted to hardtop or truck cab. Secondhand hood frames are difficult to source and expensive, though reproduction replacements are available. New replacement hoods and seats are also available.

One of the major problems with the vehicles is wear associated with almost half a century of use and indeed, abuse and corrosion.

The original 2-litre petrol engine is expensive to rebuild

THE EARLY YEARS

The Series One 88 inch is an ideal vehicle for restoration or as a weekend alternative to the euro box

and is often replaced with a later, bigger engine as a cost cutting measure. The later engine is not as good on petrol, though. Gearboxes can be upgraded to the Series III type with syncromesh on second gear, but the lack of it is no great problem. Most items can be rebuilt or reconditioned or a good second hand part substituted.

Rust is the biggest issue to address. Corrosion of the chassis outriggers and rear crossmember is common though replacement parts are available or, indeed, a newly constructed full chassis. The bulkhead also suffers badly but new top rails and footwells and other rusty bits can be replaced, as can the whole assembly.

Joining the Land Rover Series One Club is recommended as it opens the door to knowledge and information, spare parts and specialist suppliers of every day components needed to run a vehicle or major bits for a rebuild.

Older Land Rovers are not to everyone's taste, they are not

fast vehicles and unless great attention has been paid to the door seals and the like, not particularly weather tight. The heaters are not really efficient and the seats and driving position are not up to car-like standards.

in conclusion

Do not be tempted to confuse a Series One with a car, as it most definitely is not. It is a willing worker, will get you there almost as quickly as anything else though only manages approximately 60mph at full chat. They are not the best performers on motorways, though they will sit all day with the lorries in lane 1 at 50mph. They are guaranteed, however, to put the smile back on your face, as they are fun to drive.

Prices are rising slowly but steadily and at levels higher than money in the bank. Therefore, £500 will get you a restoration project and £7,000 a fully restored vehicle. If you want a tidy vehicle with a genuine MOT then £2,500-£3,500 ought to be your budget. **LRM**

CIVVY STREET
MILITARIES

The pros and cons of owning an ex-military Land Rover – what is the best option for you?

There's no reason not to buy an ex-military Land Rover, but remember that some parts and panels, like those for the 101 may be hard, if not impossible, to find.

EX-MILITARY Land Rovers make good vehicles to run. Some people are attracted to the olive drab paint scheme and are ex-military enthusiasts, others are attracted to the heavy duty, well made and maintained vehicles for future commercial use. When released by the military they were, in the past, sold by auction and bought in large numbers by numerous dealers

Many were exported to new users, some being other armed forces. Some were disposed of near to where they were used, such as in Malta, Cyprus and Germany. Now vehicles are disposed of by tender and the only practical way for an individual to buy a vehicle is from one of the dealers who buys them in bulk.

registrations

Most will be registered for you and are now issued with an age related number relating to the date the vehicle was first in service. This date is not necessarily the date of manufacture as vehicles were often stored for several years unused before issue. This is especially true with 101s.

At one point, almost everything was given a 'Q' plate as being of indeterminate age and, up to 1983, vehicles were given whatever was current at the time. For most ex-military vehicles, the date of manufacture, age of registration letter and date of registration are not the same thing, though will be in this chronological order. It is possible to get an age related number on a Q or other vehicle registration that seems the wrong age.

As a 'hobby' vehicle, the more esoteric models such as the 101 or Lightweight are fine, as time can be taken for repairs and getting spares. The 24V vehicles are cheaper because of their complexity and are also best avoided unless you want an authentic radio vehicle. If you want to run one as an everyday vehicle, then a 90 or 110 would probably be the better bet. Many hide their military history and it might just be the fire extinguisher and data plate that alerts the owner to a previous life.

The best place to look for an ex-military Land Rover is from one of the dealers who advertise in **LRM**, or from a private ad in the classifieds. Internet auction sites such as eBay or through the Land Rover club applicable to your intended purchase (see **LRM**'s club listings) are also possible locations to find a vehicle.

Check for condition, as a service life of ten or 15 years, plus anything up to 40 years in civvy street, will have taken a toll on the vehicle. More recent releases might have been in a war, or even two, or peace keeping duties overseas or on an airbase in the UK. It is the condition of the chassis and other mechanical bits that is important and not the age or the shiny paintwork.

As for prices, they have always been higher than a similar age civilian vehicle. Years ago it was perhaps justified to pay a premium for a low mileage, well maintained vehicle, but now it is difficult to see why a hand painted 90 with no power steering sliding windows and an old 2.5 engine is worth twice as much as a similar age Tdi powered, power steering, shiny painted one with wind up windows.

Running an ex-military vehicle is no problem at all. Most service items are readily available through non-franchised and military specialists. A lot of components can be bought from the manufacturer, though it is best if you have the part numbers when you visit the dealer. Body spares for the 101 and Lightweight are no longer manufactured, but secondhand, and the odd 'new old' stock bits, can be found.

If, then, military green is your thing, there is no reason not to buy an ex-military Land Rover. **LRM**

CLASSIC PARTS

SPOILT FOR **CHOICE**

It is vital you know what you need when looking to purchase a station wagon – too many variables can make it a difficult decision

WITH SO many sorts of station wagon type vehicles on offer from Land Rover and many of them subdivided into several distinct different models, the prospective purchaser of a vehicle has to decide what is really suitable for their requirements.

You really do need to list down the things you want the vehicle to do, what you expect from it, what features are needed on the vehicle and how much money you have to spend. I cannot emphasise how important this process is. If you do not get this bit right, you will probably buy a Land Rover that is not the right one for you. Be truthful with the answers as you can quite easily distort the results and need and want can be confused.

How many people do you need to carry? Do you need to tow anything, if so, how heavy? How many miles will it do a year? Will you do many long journeys in it? Do you need an automatic? How much money have you to spend on it. Will you enjoy owning it?

In some cases you can tick all

the boxes, often with more than one type of vehicle. In others, there may be only one and that might not be a perfect match, and there might not even be a vehicle that fits at all if you have too many inflexible trivial requirements.

Some answers might suggest alternatives. For example, if you only do 3-5,000 miles a year, the lower purchase price and maintenance and fuel cost of a petrol engine will probably be better than a diesel. If you do 15,000 miles a year, the higher miles per gallon would suggest you need a diesel or an LPG conversion.

If you need seven seats, a Defender or Discovery will fulfil the requirement, but if you need an automatic as well as the seven seats, then only a Discovery will be available to you.

This is why you need to set down your requirements so that you can buy a Land Rover that is the best fit for your purpose.

Once you have sorted out suitable models, price will limit you further. If, for example, you only have £2,000 to spend, you will not buy a Freelander or P38A Range Rover, so it is a waste of time looking for one.

careful inspection
When you have found what you want, look at it very carefully or get it looked at by a genuinely knowledgeable person. Unless it is only a few years old, corrosion can be a major problem.

Some types are more susceptible than others and in different places. Find out where to look on the vehicle you want. Some engines have particular problems, some being related to the build date of the vehicle. Some gearboxes have particular problems, as well, so find out what to look for.

Once you have bought your Station Wagon, whatever it is,

look after it. Don't forget to service it – you can never spend too much money on rust and corrosion preventative measures. You will be repaid with a longer vehicle life and/or higher residual value.

Do not forget to do the routine maintenance on time. Oil changes, timing belt replacement and all other routine jobs have time or mileages when they need doing by the manufacturer. If you want a long term, reliable vehicle they should be regarded as compulsory and not optional. Check that the previous owners have been as careful as you intend to be. It is nice to see a big file of invoices with a vehicle for servicing and work done previously, especially if you have not had to pay them.

Defenders, Station Wagons in the purest form, are usually in better condition than the commercial versions. Beware, though, as many of the 90 versions on sale have been converted from a commercial version part way through their life and may not have all the features of a line-built example, such as sound deadening, heated rear window, and so on. **LRM**

Manufacturer's specifications need to be the best fit possible for your requirements. Make certain of the previous history of seven seat 90 Station Wagons as many are later conversions from vans.

WORK HORSE

Dependability and character are the calling cards of every Land Rover Defender

THE DEFENDER is a fantastic vehicle for working in and that is just what most are used for. They soak up the work with ease, but it often leaves some tell-tale signs that will show up for future purchasers or users.

Corrosion is a major worry to look out for, especially the rear of the chassis and the top corners of the front bulkhead. Repair is possible and, if properly done, is not a problem. The engines are long lasting but there is a timing belt issue with some ages of the 300 Tdi and both Tdi engines are known to crack cylinder heads. All diesels need belt replacement at the correct mileages or age. Many of the Tdi engines are well past the 200,000 miles point with no trouble. The V8 is a long lasting trouble free unit, if a little thirsty, but most V8 vehicles are not

high mileage and are in better condition than similar diesels. Lpg conversions suit this engine and type of vehicle very well.

The 2.5 petrol and 2.5 diesels, fitted to special order in vehicles such as the military Defenders up until the Tdi gained MOD approval, are relatively trouble free. All gearboxes can be reluctant when down changing as they wear and there are wear problems with the mainshaft on the LT77 box that were cured by the use of a cross drilled gear for better lubrication. The R380 does not have this problem, but does suffer changing problems as it wears.

While time, use and abuse take their toll, most problems, even major ones, will not leave you stranded as the vehicles will usually get home unaided.

The main problem when buying a vehicle is getting value for money. There are many vehicles out there that have

A couple of new side wings and this could fetch a decent price

had a hard life initially and are tarted up with a new wing or two, some seats and a respray and sold on for top money. They do have a value, but it's not usually the asking price. Proper 90 Station Wagon Defenders are rare and only the real thing is worth top money. The 7th letter in the VIN ought to be 'B' for a 90 SW. If it is an 'A', then it was built as a van or pick up.

Water leaks into the body through the roof are common. The lack of a sunroof and alpine windows gives less potential for leaking, but the sealing between the roof components often dries out and water is drawn in. Resealing the roof works, but not easily when it is wet.

All the doors are prone to rotting. The driver's one is

particularly prone to failure as the greater use encourages corrosion, but getting a replacement is simple, if a little expensive. Most problems are visible or show up on a road test, so finding a good one is a matter of a good inspection.

The Defender, illustrated above, with a couple of new wings, a couple of seat cushions a bit of TLC and a coat of paint, would fetch, as a seven year old vehicle, about £8,000 and if it were converted to County Station Wagon spec, the asking price might even go as high as £12,000. If you are spending this sort of money on a vehicle, it is essential to ascertain what it has been doing in a previous life. **LRM**

Is the Defender cheap to run?
Running costs are quite low, insurance is cheaper than a Discovery or Range Rover and spares are inexpensive if you shop around.

Driving experience
Fine if you regard it as the utility vehicle that it is. The up spec trim and so on does not get away from the fact that it is a working vehicle. The 110 is a better tow vehicle and obviously has more internal space than a 90. It also rides better on the road with little or no fuel penalty. Parking is not much more difficult.

Problems
No, I was very careful in buying a good one. The only surprise it has sprung in three years other than routine brake pads and so on is the 300 Tdi engine cracking the cylinder head which cost £750 in total to replace.

Replacement
Another Defender of course but as mine has been properly rust-proofed from an early age and I look after it properly I feel it has a long life yet.

EVER READY

Looking for a used Discovery? Les Roberts shows you what to expect from your new purchase

THE OLDEST are now well into their teens and old enough to party on their own. Like most teenagers, they can be really problematic and have tantrums.

One of the most obvious points to look out for is corrosion. The body skin is mostly aluminium, but that corrodes readily, especially where it is next to steel. The doors, all five of them, and rear wings are favourite points for this bubbly corrosion.

The rear inner floor also rots out as does the rear body crossmember. Leaking sunroofs and Alpine window seals contribute to the corrosion and it also helps the trim to change shape and fall apart. Misted windows are a tell-tale sign of a damp interior.

The side opening rear door is great for putting things into the vehicle. Many have been used semi commercially and bear the bruises on the trim as proof.

All five speed boxes have problems. The early LT77 have syncro problems and a wear failure of the rear output shaft. Revised lubrication sorted that out, but the R380 box can still be agricultural changing gear. The 200Tdi is prone to the front pulley coming loose and a big batch of the 300Tdi engines were prone to timing belt problems, and fuel pump problems, though most of the timing belt issues ought to have been resolved by now. Both diesels can crack cylinder heads.

The V8 is the best engine for reliability if you can live with the fuel costs commensurate with about 15mpg and the gearboxes seem to fare better when there is a petrol engine in front of them. The diesels do 25-30mpg with the older pre-catalyst and exhaust gas recirculating 200Tdi being best. Automatic boxes, while great to drive, do lower the mpg by as much as 10 percent and about the same amount from performance figures.

On the plus side, the Discovery is very versatile. You can fit seven people if you have the extra two jump seats in the back or a wardrobe inside and tow another 3.5 tons if you wish. They are ideal for leisure activities with people or anything that involves towing a caravan or boat or horse box.

Off-road, the departure and approach angles are good, and events such as the Camel Trophy, showed just where a standard specification vehicle could go. As prices tumble more and more, people are beginning to use this aspect of their ability.

One of the biggest problems, when buying a Discovery is working out what it is worth as there are so many different models and trim levels. For example, a Tdi five door cost £21,300 in 1995 and the top model five door cost £27,000 at the same time (26% more). This is still reflected in the value. The base model M reg is worth, say £7000, at a dealer and the ES probably £8500 (21 percent more)

As well as the good ones, there are plenty of horrible Discoverys out there waiting for the unsuspecting purchaser and a proper inspection by someone who is familiar with the vehicles ought to be mandatory.

If you're buying privately or without a warranty, do not spend up to your limit as, if trouble ever occurs with the engine or gearbox, it is usually a four figure bill. As many vehicles are well past the 100,000 mileage mark, one would expect these older vehicles to be more problematical. A bill for £1000 to fix the engine on a £2000 G reg vehicle is a lot, especially as it is still only worth £2000 in working order.

From £1500 to £15000, the Discovery is still a very worthwhile vehicle. **LRM**

If you were to ask the following questions of the typical Discovery owner, these would be the answers.

Is the Discovery cheap to run?
Fuel and routine maintenance is quite cheap

How would you describe your driving experience?
The high roof and space behind the driver is a bit van like, but like a van it will carry anything. The high centre of gravity takes a bit of getting used to.

Have you had many problems?
No, the timing belt was sorted out under warranty as was the dashboard.

When the time comes, what will you replace it with?
I would guess it will be another Discovery as, once one has become accustomed to owning such a competent vehicle, it is difficult to think of anything else that will do the job. Defenders or Range Rovers would not suit my needs.

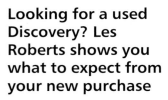

SECOND GENERATION

Though still a 'new' vehicle, the Series II Discovery is now affordable and is good value

THE DISCOVERY Series II is not a bad buy secondhand. It is an excellent family vehicle with proper seating for seven if needed. The models with all the toys are a pleasure to drive on and off the road. Fuel consumption excepted, the V8 auto is the best vehicle to drive but the more frugal diesel is more popular and fetches more money for a similar vehicle.

Automatics are also worth about £1,000 more than a manual. The option of the extra two seats in the back can add as much as £1,000 to the value as well and the more heavily specified vehicles are more desirable. However, if there are extra toys fitted there is potentially more to go wrong.

With similar age vehicles being, in some cases, more than £12,000 more expensive when they were new, make certain the price you are paying reflects the level of equipment that ought to be fitted.

As a new purchaser you did better to put your money into a Discovery in 1998 than into a Range Rover as you would have 38% of it left, whereas the Range Rover owner would only have 28%. This can be looked at in a different way with second-hand vehicles as it can be argued the Range Rover is better value for the same sum now, as it cost substantially more when it was new.

The popularity of the Discovery in its market sector keeps the price up. If you can manage without all the complicated toys such as climate control and cruise control and the extra seats, then you can drive a hard bargain. If it has got steel wheels as well, then it ought to be a snip.

The Discovery found favour with several commercial users. Police specification vehicles offered as good a performance as Range Rovers for a lot less money. Other commercial users found favour with the economically attractive van version that has black glass to the rear of the driver and only two seats. They are hard to spot as they just look like a normal one with privacy glass. The vans are not that plentiful on the secondhand scene and only really make sense if just two seats will suffice and you are VAT registered. They do make a useful alternative to a Defender, especially if you carry clean goods or need automatic transmission.

The manual gearbox can wear and be a bit clunky on the changes but the auto is usually a well proven design. Engine-wise, the V8 can suffer water problems and even cracked blocks, and the diesel is quite reliable now that the teething problems have been ironed out. There can be problems with some of the ancillary items with radiators, in particular not lasting as long as one might expect.

Corrosion is not really much of an issue as the electrolytic areas have been designed out and the manufacturer has striven to improve build quality over the previous vehicle.

The ABS system is prone to playing up and the air suspension can cause problems, including premature failure of the air bags.

High mileage early vehicles with low specification can be found for less than £9,000 but you need to really be paying £13-14,000 upwards to get a worthwhile vehicle. Always look for a proper service history as it is important. The diesel needs a service at 6,000 miles and the V8 at 12,000, but it will do them both good if you want to keep them for long to reduce the oil change intervals. **LRM**

LAND ROVER'S
BABY

As older models come to the market the Freelander is falling into everyone's range

THE COST of purchasing a Freelander is getting lower all the time. The oldest, 'R' registration 1997 models, are still fetching around the £5000 mark at 60,000 miles. Many have done a lot more miles but still seem to retain a high asking price.

In terms of value, five doors are worth more than three doors and diesels more than petrol. Early models with no HDC or ETC are hard to sell, as are some colours, especially white.

The later vehicles had a new diesel engine, the Td4, a common rail turbocharged unit bought in from BMW. It is a far more civilised vehicle than the older diesel and well worth stretching for if possible, the cheapest being around £10,000. There is a shortage of vehicles on offer in the nearly new bracket as, with the many finance options on offer, most

owners keep the vehicles for three years and then move them on. 2001 'X' are now turning up more readily for £12-15,000. The excellent Steptronic automatic gearbox ought to make the vehicle worth some £1000 more than a manual vehicle.

Always look for a proper full service record for all vehicles with possibly an independent specialist or local garage taking over as the vehicle ages. Look for regular mileage increments as a Freelander can be 'clocked' for as little as £80, which is a lot less then extra mileage penalties on lease vehicles.

Problems have occurred on earlier vehicles but most have been resolved and sorted under warranty. High rates of tyre wear were sorted by revising the tyre pressures, Michelin-shod vehicles did not seem to suffer as much as other makes. Rear differentials can fail but usually before

50,000 miles. There can be problems with the rear drive-shaft bearings as well.

Engine wise, the diesels are generally OK but there have been head problems with the 1.8 petrol, though most were sorted under warranty.

Body wise, there are not many problems, though the window lift cables can snap on high-use vehicles. There are not many electrical gremlins, though as with any modern vehicle, the more that is fitted the more opportunity there is for things to go wrong.

Corrosion does not seem to be an issue yet, but with many plastic panels, wings bumpers and no traditional electrolytic potential problems from aluminium and steel joints, they ought to be rust free for a long time. The manufacturer has also made a good job of rust prevention both passively by designing

out mud traps and the like, and actively by sealing seams and waxing internal cavities. If you are thinking of long term ownership then they will always take more rust preventing wax.

Running one could not be easier. They all do 30mpg and more except for the automatic-only V6 engine; the Td4 auto is less economical than the manual.

Insurance groups range from 8 to 12 depending on engine type.

Body style is up to the individual. Some might hanker after a three-door soft or hard top to remove the back for summer motoring. For many, the five-door estate is most useful and the most prolific model, but for you it might be a Td4 van with Steptronic transmission that fits the bill.

Whatever you choose you won't be disappointed. **LRM**

Is the Freelander cheap to run?
Fuel economy is most un-Land Rover like at around 30mpg. Servicing and tyres are not expensive and, other than consumables such as brake pads and tyres, we have not had to replace anything on either of the two we have owned.

Driving experience
The command driving position and height makes it easy to get in and out of and visibility is good all round. On the road it is light and nippy to drive with very positive handling. It corners as well as most front wheel drive cars but, when the going gets tough, its mountain goat characteristics take over and it will drive where it is almost impossible to walk, it is incredible. Those who have not pushed theirs towards the limit, not that I have found the limit of ours yet, do not know what they are missing.

Problems
The first one we had had a new petrol engine under warranty at 60,000 miles but was still running fine at 100,000+ when we sold it. The driver's window lift cables also broke. Our current Td4 Steptronic has been fine so far over 25,000 miles.

AUTOMATICALLY BETTER BY FAR

The automatic is a good choice of Land Rover – as long as you know what to look out for

AUTOMATIC TRANSMISSION, in the minds of many people, is for the old or infirm who cannot manage to use a normal gearbox. They could not be more wrong in this perception. Driving on the road is much safer with an auto as both hands can be kept on the steering wheel and all concentration can be put into driving and not diverted to working the clutch and gearbox.

Indeed, many high speed Police, Fire and Ambulance vehicles are automatic transmission for this reason. Towing is easier, as well, as the vehicle is always in the right ratio for the conditions. Cooling used to be an issue with automatic cars when towing, but Land Rover's products have sufficient cooling to cope with their maximum tow weights as standard.

Off the road, autos are better than manuals, both in standard vehicles and in the powerful off-road racing vehicles. The gearing is always right for the job, the power is fed in more progressively, so wheel spin and loss of traction are reduced, and two hands can be kept on the steering wheel.

good selection

If you want an automatic, either because of need or choice, then there are quite a high proportion of Range Rovers and Discoverys in that format. You will have to pay a premium of between £600 and £1,000 over the price of an identical manual vehicle because they are more desirable and, in many cases, cost extra when new.

You will also have to pay for the auto in fuel costs, as well. This is not so much of a problem on more recent vehicles, but the old Range Rover three speed was especially poor in relation to a similar manual. The automatics work well with diesels as the torque characteristics of modern diesel engines is well suited to an automatic box and, while the 0-60 time may be reduced on paper, in reality, it matters little.

Always check out the gearbox before you finally commit to buying a vehicle. Road test it to make certain it has all the gears it should and that there is not more slipping than there ought to be. Check the box kicks down when given full throttle though, if it does not, it is usually too many carpets under the pedal or a stretched kick down cable needing adjustment.

Look at the oil on the gearbox dip stick. It should be clear red and have a smell, but not of burning. If the fluid is discoloured or brown then buy another vehicle as this is the first sign of the clutch packs or bands breaking up – a breakdown with a big bill is just around the corner. If you do not know what it looks like or smells like, tip a bit out of a top up bottle. It should always look like it has just come out of a bottle.

Repairs are best left to an expert who has the special tooling and knowledge, though a service exchange unit is easy to fit and may be done DIY. The boxes respond well to servicing and that is quite an easy job to remove the sump and fit a new filter and refill with new fluid.

long life

Auto boxes are less prone to breakages than manual boxes and many vehicles will finish their lives with the same one they had in new, untouched. They are less prone to other problems as well, like the mainshaft wear on the LT77 manual box. They also do not have the clutch arm failures common on manual Discoverys and Range Rovers.

All things considered, an automatic Land Rover is well worth a look next time you replace your vehicle. **LRM**

DEMOBBED

Land Rover fans in search of an ex-military model need look no further than WSV's impressive 600-acre airfield site

by
Bob Morrison
photography
Nick Dimbleby

READERS OF **LRM** don't need to be told that the classic Land Rover lives a much longer and fuller life than almost any other motor vehicle, and twenty or even thirty year old examples are still a relatively common sight, particularly in rural areas. The armed forces keep their vehicles longer than most, but even they pension most Land Rovers off by the time they reach their mid teens, when the money required to keep them in full fighting order usually starts to outweigh their residual value.

To the farmer, small contractor or enthusiast who, unlike the civil service bean counters, is more prepared to lavish time and effort on keeping a vehicle going, there is still plenty of life left in these old warhorses. These days, Witham Specialist Vehicles of Colsterworth in Lincolnshire are the people who bring pre-owned military Land Rovers and future owners together.

When the UK Ministry of Defence procured almost eight thousand of the Defender HS, or Wolf, model in January 1996, to replace its frontline light and medium utility truck fleet, it found itself with a bit of a problem. As a result of the collapse of the Warsaw Pact and the ending of the Cold War, Britain's armed forces had been considerably slimmed down, and not only were

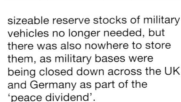

Main: Spoilt for choice – just a fraction of the demobbed Land Rover fleet being sold off by Witham SV.
Inset: A typical 'tidied-up' ex-military Ninety.

sizeable reserve stocks of military vehicles no longer needed, but there was also nowhere to store them, as military bases were being closed down across the UK and Germany as part of the 'peace dividend'.

In 1997, the remaining leaf sprung Land Rovers were finally confirmed as being excess to requirements. It was decided that the easiest way to get rid of them, while also getting some return for the taxpayer, was to hand them over to a single agent for disposal on behalf of the Crown.

The original utility truck tender, issued towards the end of 1991, had called for the new vehicle to be introduced over a five year period but, by the time the order was placed, the MoD had come to an arrangement with Land Rover to have the entire fleet manufactured in just eighteen months. Although payment for the contract would still be spread over a long period, the

significantly shortened manufacture phase better suited Land Rover's production schedules, allowing cost savings that would compensate for the longish payment plan. The armed forces would also benefit by getting the long-awaited Series III replacements in one clean sweep.

Everyone was happy, with the exception of the civil servants, who suddenly had several thousand very old Land Rovers to get shot of all at once. Since the end of WWII, it had become standard practice to auction off quantities of vehicles and equipment at various depots around the country, in later years using commercial auction houses for the job. However, it was clear to all that this system was no longer viable for the vast quantity of Land Rovers about to be demobbed.

The very youngest of these leaf-sprung Land Rovers was almost fourteen years old by the time of disposal and some ▶

Centre: Variations on a theme. Hard, soft, short, long, extended or ambulance – the choice is yours. Bottom left: Range Rover 6x4 crash tenders are Nick's favourite. Bottom right: Distinctive front bumper of Locomotors 127 Ambulance.

others were over twenty, so it was clear that there was no way they were going to be worth anything much if all dumped on the market at the one time.

The solution that the Government came up with was to appoint a disposal agent to take the entire fleet, possibly numbering as many as five thousand vehicles, off their hands in one go to drip feed them to the market. Military Vehicle Spares who, as their name suggests, were originally contracted to dispose of assorted spares on behalf of the Ministry of Defence, were given an additional contract to handle the Series Land Rovers, and their disused airfield in Staffordshire suddenly became the world's biggest secondhand Land Rover car park.

early coilers

Five years down the line from the Series sell-off, the last of the Wolves had made its way through the system to the end users. Additionally, the so-called white

Above: Civilian door trim on very early Ninety 25KD13. Above right: Headlight trim on 25KD13 is non-military and bumper looks like a late Series III military pattern. Below: Rapier Tractor (left) has longer wheelbase and wider body than One-Ten, plus it's V8-powered.

fleet principle, where rear echelon Land Rovers are leased to the MoD by a civilian supplier rather than being bought outright, was now in full swing. Bob Weir touched on this subject last month in his article on the mixed RAF Leuchars fleet of 'green' military specification and 'white' civilian specification Land Rovers.

Due to these introductions and changes, the MoD now had a large quantity of mid-eighties military specification Ninety and One-Ten model Land Rovers surplus to requirements. This is where Witham Specialist Vehicles entered the story.

Last year, a fixed term contract for the disposal of all wheeled vehicles and plant was put out to tender and, after intense competition, Withams were appointed sole disposal agents. Their mission statement, in line with current Government policy, is "to ensure that the extended working life of MoD vehicles is maximised".

Withams are no newcomers to

the Land Rover business and have been selling surplus military and specialist vehicles and plant for more than thirty years. Under the old auction system, they would travel around the UK and Continent buying up batches of surplus vehicles, returning them to their 600 acre former wartime airfield site on the Lincolnshire/Rutland border. Here they would refurbish the vehicles where necessary, and sell them on to both fleet and civilian buyers.

Such was their marketing prowess, that they even managed to shift old helicopters. Any visit to their well-ordered vehicle pool could be guaranteed to turn up the odd surprise or two; case in point being the white 130 Comms body covered in my column last month.

The company has always been a family-run business, turning from a partnership to a limited company twenty-one years ago. Even though today it is the biggest in its field, that family atmosphere is still evident when you visit – even the dog strolls out to greet familiar visi-

tors. More to the point though, senior management Paul and Doug are Land Rover people – with Landy as a surname Doug really had no alternative.

Their private vehicle collections, which are tucked away out of sight, include a number of unique Land Rovers as well as historic armoured vehicles, and Paul's secret Series One is an absolute jewel. One day I hope to persuade him to dust her

down and bring her out into the light – though as he has an aversion to cleaning his own vehicles, that might take some time.

His private vehicle collection may be gathering dust, but the same cannot be said for the ex-MoD fleet. Although the vehicles are stowed in regimented rows around the vast yard at Colsterworth when they first arrive, at least one of each specific model type is available in forecourt condition at all times, for those who want to turn up and buy on the spot.

Some of these forecourt vehicles will only have required a basic valet service. Others will have had a full mechanical overhaul and been re-

Above left: Green patches betray that this Rapier Tractor once sported a winch. Right: Locomotors-bodied ambulances have angular front roof. Below, clockwise from left: Military Ninety hard top rear light cluster; speed limits for Wolf drivers, 25KD13 has wind-up windows; 200 kph seems a bit optimistic for a diesel Land Rover.

sprayed to look almost as good as new. In line with their mission statement, they will sell either in 'as seen' condition or fully refurbished to maximise the return to the taxpayer while still shifting vehicles as fast as possible. The last thing the MoD needs is large numbers of vehicles corroding away unsold.

Incidentally, it is the man from the Ministry who sets the guide price for each individual vehicle, not Withams, and their prime function is to get maximum return against this figure. However, as they know the secondhand Land Rover market inside out, they would never consider passing off a bag of nails as anything other than what it is. Likewise, they realise the true value of a well-maintained, low mileage, late model V8 Defender. You may well pick up a bargain, but you won't get a steal.

business as usual
When Nick and I visited Withams in February it was a typical day, with a constant stream of customers arriving in the yard, prepared vehicles being collected by purchasers, a Land Rover in the paint shop, another on the ramps in the workshop, and two deliveries ▶

of badly crash-damaged Wolves due for arrival around lunch time. The team were as busy as usual, and only had a few minutes to spare for a chat in between dealing with customers but, as we have both known them for many years, they were prepared to trust us with the keys to anything in the yard or forecourt that we wanted to take for a spin. Maybe that is why our intended three hour visit stretched out to seven. We were like kids in a sweet shop.

On a brief cruise around the premises Doug pointed out a couple of rare machines that only a keen eye would spot. I had already pinged the Defence Research Agency early One-Ten hard top, which I am sure would have a few stories to tell but for the Official Secrets Act. The pair of Defender

Above left: The hard top Ninety is by far the most popular ex-MoD model. Above right: Pioneer tools on hard top door. Below, left to right: Ambulances tend to be in extremely good condition; illuminated sign over windscreen and occulting beacon; camo One-Ten on one of the maintenance bay ramps.

110 CSW dog vehicles, used by the Defence Police Service also caught my eye, as I browsed around the forecourt. However, it was only when Doug pointed out that a rather nondescript Ninety soft top had carried the registration 25KD13, that I paid closer attention to it. The letter D in the number marks this one out as being in service in 1985, which is before the main batch was manufactured, and it could well be one of the Trials vehicles. A closer look was definitely in order.

The first thing which struck me about 25KD13 was the one-piece side windows, though the doors themselves have the horizontal trim strip normally found on two-piece military doors. Up close, it became apparent that the doors are single piece and the windows are of the

civilian wind-down type. Internal door trim is also civilian style, with golf-tee lock buttons. The other noticeable thing inside is that three civvy-style seats are fitted, and there is every indication that these are original fit. However, the dash-board is clearly derived from the early military spec One-Ten.

Externally, the headlight surrounds and lack of bonnet hold-down clips suggest civilian specification, but the front bumper is clearly of Series III military origin, with holes for upper extensions, though it also has the towing pin found on some later military spec vehicles. Interestingly, the filler cap is also of Series III design. I suspect that this Land Rover may actually have been conceived for rear echelon, possibly RAF, use and it may even be one of a small interim

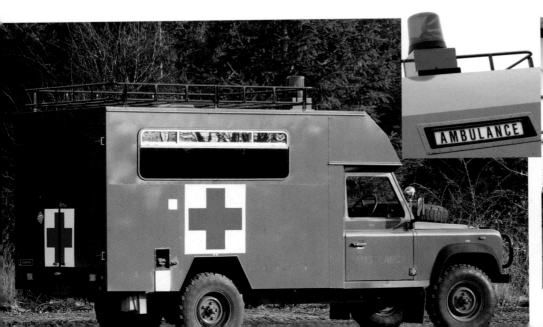

purchase batch rather than a Trials prototype. More research is definitely needed into the background of this one.

too good to play with

After a good wander around both yard and forecourt, plus a visit to the paint shop, Nick and I decided to take just five vehicles, and a spare to use as a camera platform, round to the disused runway alongside Witham's off-road demonstration course. Had the vehicles we picked not been in top condition, we might have been tempted to have a play on the circuit, but this would have been unfair on the buyers, given my reputation for breaking things. As it was, we lost one of the five by mid-afternoon, as

a buyer had decided it was the one for him.

The famous five that we picked to photograph were the early Ninety soft top, a 1987 production batch Ninety hard top, a production One-Ten soft top from around the same time, a late eighties One-Two-Seven Rapier Tractor and an early nineties Defender 127 ambulance.

This last vehicle was one of the two later batches with bodies produced by Locomotors, but Witham also had a few of the earlier Marshall-bodied ambulances for sale as well. The Rapier Tractor still sported a coat of sandy paint, as well as the stencilled logo of the RAF Tactical Communications Wing on one side, but internal fittings and the front-mounted Warn

Above, clockwise from top left: Yellow ex-RAF window hard top One-Ten; no longer up to Aviation Authority standards, these Range Rovers have lost much of their value; the ambulance is interesting to drive; ambulance interior; One-Ten soft tops are less popular than little brother. Below: Rapier Tractor and Ambulance share same extended 127 wheelbase.

winch had long gone. Possibly the paint job was done for Exercise Bright Star in Egypt or Exercise Saif Sareea in Oman, as the Rapier Tractor was not used in the 1991 Gulf War.

After the airfield shoot, during which I took the opportunity to go for a run with blues and twos on – well, it would have been rude not to – we took our little convoy back to the main yard in two batches and started delving deeper among the rows of parked toys. Nick, who has been a Range Rover nut since he was in short trousers, went off to gaze fondly at the TACR2 crash rescue tenders, while I squirmed in among the Defenders looking for unusual markings and add-ons.

It may seem to be a bit anorakish to some, but it is only by examining every military Land Rover for fine detail, with the eye of train or plane spotter, that we can write with any authority on our specialist topic, and in Witham's yard there is detail aplenty. Fortunately, Paul and Doug have known us long enough to trust us out there on our own, but on health and safety grounds alone, they cannot let casual visitors browse in the way that used to be possible in days gone by. They are also busy men, and have no time to spare for time-wasters, who Paul seems to be able to sense even before they turn into the long drive that leads to the sales office.

taken a bashing

Having seen all that was to be seen, we met up at the Wolf graveyard to examine the amount of damage that these Land Rovers can soak up. Over the last two decades, I have seen more than my fair share

Above, clockwise from left: Badly trashed Wolves; more accident damaged Wolves arrive by truck; the sales team with Doug in the middle; last of the Lightweights Below: Having fun with all lights blazing.

of trashed Land Rovers, so it was interesting to note how the heavily strengthened Wolf compares.

When I first saw the amount of additional metalwork that the Chertsey boffins were demanding for Wolf, I must admit that I thought it was a bit over the top. However, the Wolf of 1998 is a much more powerful beast than the Series II of 1958, even though the external body shape is virtually unchanged, and it is clear that the strength changes were necessary.

No way could a Series Land Rover sustain as much accident damage as some of these Wolves, yet still retain the basic passenger envelope integrity. However, next time I am a passenger in the rear of one I will definitely be using the seat belts provided, as seeing the damage that can be caused in a rollover at speed is quite sobering.

No doubt one or two of you are considering buying a written-off Wolf for restoration, but at this point I must warn you that it is not that simple. These vehicles are released as being beyond economical repair, and as such they come with no paperwork that could be used to put them back on the road. Not only that, but the terms of sale set out by the

Government mean that it is not possible to cannibalise any of the vehicles for parts. If you want to mix and match, you will have to buy complete vehicles, even if this means buying a whole vehicle for, say, one axle, which could be rather expensive. It is also worth noting that the computer-designed Wolf chassis is constructed to take out some of the force of an accident in a way which earlier designs did not, so finding a crash damaged vehicle with a repairable chassis will not be easy.

In addition to the vehicles which Witham are selling off on behalf of the MoD, they also have a wide range of other Land Rovers from their own separate stocks of surplus. If the latest release ex-military Defender is beyond your budget, they also have a varied range of leaf sprung Land Rovers for sale, including some Dutch diesels, either as seen or fully refurbished. They also occasionally get in some interesting bits and pieces from other Government sources, both British and foreign, so a regular browse at their website may be worthwhile. **LRM**

Check out *www.witham-sv.com* you may be surprised.

WHAT HAPPENED TO THAT FAVOURITE OLD LANDY?
WHO OWNED YOURS BEFORE YOU?

LET YOUR SEARCH BEGIN...

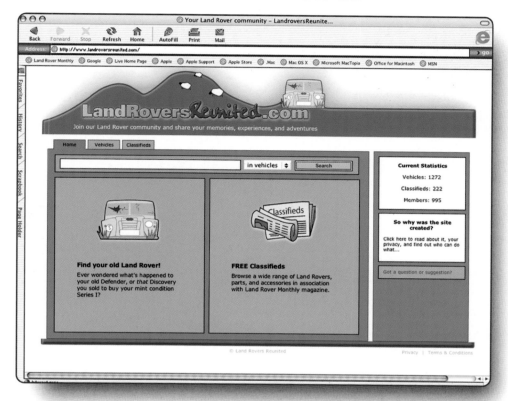

- ## ■ BROWSE FOR YOUR OLD VEHICLE & FIND THE PRESENT OWNER

- ## ■ ENTER YOUR VEHICLE'S HISTORY FOR OTHERS TO READ

- ## ■ OTHER MEMBERS CAN TELL YOU MORE ABOUT YOUR LANDY

- ## ■ FREE CLASSIFIED SECTION

- ## ■ FREE MEMBERSHIP

LandRoversReunited.com
TOGETHER WE CAN BUILD THE WORLD'S BIGGEST LAND ROVER COMMUNITY

TOP DEFENDER

Does Land Rover's flagship Defender make sense against the rest of the range from Solihull?

by
John Henderson

THE 110 XS Station Wagon is Land Rover's Defender flagship, packing all the options in the book, plus nine seats, into a long passenger body and costing £1,000 more than the even longer 130 County Double Cab.

At £27,995 it is also £2,400 more than the equivalent Defender 90, though because it is legally a minibus, businesses can claim back the VAT making it £1,931 cheaper than the 90 (see 'Catch the Bus' panel). The extra buys 43.4cm more in the wheelbase and an extra 71.6cm in length. To my eyes its length makes it look more dated, perhaps because a 90 is closer to a modern hatchback shape. But what advantages and disadvantages does this extra length give you apart from two more doors and three more seats?

Surprisingly, the 110 Station Wagon is 106mm shorter than a Discovery II and weighs about

Above: With metallic paint and alloy whels, the XS Defender is a far cry from the workhorse of old. Inset: Not much to see but plenty of power.

180kg less. Its long, straight roof probably helps to make it look longer from the outside than the Discovery's stepped roof. It also looks longer on the inside because you are looking down a tube towards a rear window half the size of a Discovery's. This also affects your view of the world, even when compared with looking through the same sized rear window in a 90, because your angle of sight over the spare wheel is shallower, so your rear vision is much more restricted. The 110 also feels big to drive. Its turning circle is half a metre more than a 90's so it needs more space between trees to get about, but not excessively so. When it is on the open road you are more aware of its bulk, mostly because it takes the edge off its agility. Turn in is more blunt than with a 90 XS, which has anti-roll bars, or Discovery. Body roll is not excessive but it is slow to

return after it has leaned, so on a series of bends the body movement is slightly behind the chassis in a way you don't get with a 90 or Discovery.

This is made worse by a total lack of steering feel. We've commented before on how Defenders with the Freestyle option wheels, which are standard on XS models, don't seem to have as good a steering feel as those on standard rubber but this 110 XS felt less reassuring than the 90XS we featured in May 2003 and is big to drive on a wet road by guesswork.

But there is a major benefit to having extra length: the ride. The 110 Station Wagon smoothes out humps and dips in a way that would shame even some more ostentatious non-Land Rover off-roaders. It greatly reduces pitching on poor roads and tracks while on decent roads, especially at high speeds, it virtually eliminates it.

This makes its cruising stance much less active than a 90's and therefore more comfortable and less tiring. It also means the 110 feels an even more stable and reassuring towcar than the 90 with outfit pitching reduced to a level the 90 can only achieve with a

blade stabiliser. However, on roads with edge subsidence it had a distinct sideways twitch at speed, made more unnerving by the poor steering feel.

Like all Defenders, it has very long travel coil suspension. It is capable of absorbing big holes with ease and in the 110 the typical live axle shudder is much less pronounced than in a 90. Yet it is also well controlled enough to come back from the effects of a hump without bounce or float.

This combination of well controlled long travel and the 110's resistance to pitching mean you can drive rough tracks in surprising comfort at significantly higher speeds than some luxury off-roaders manage. In fact, it was much more comfortable on local 'drove roads' than an air-sprung Lexus RX300 I had the week before.

Mud was in short supply during the test because the East Anglian soil had had little rain so it quickly soaked up any moisture. But on greasy tracks and in deep, tractor churned soft soil the 110 had much better directional stability than a 90 on the same tyres. But when things get really tough, a 90 is bound to be more capable with its much shorter rear overhang giving it a 53 degree departure angle against the 110's 34 degrees and its shorter wheelbase improving the ramp breakover angle by three degrees.

performance aplenty

The 110's size did not blunt the Td5 turbodiesel's performance as much as I had expected. In Defender form the Td5 develops 122bhp at

At home on rough tracks or roads and there's no shortage of horsepower for towing a box

4,200rpm and 221lbft of torque at 1,950rpm, against the Discovery Td5's 136bhp and similar torque. However, the lower weight of the 110 means its 60.4bhp per tonne power to weight ratio is little over two per cent down on the Discovery's.

At lower speeds the two are probably quite close in perfor-mance, though the 90 is much more sprightly than either but, as speeds increase, the Defender 110 runs out of puff much earlier, so by 60mph its performance is starting to lose its edge while the lighter 90 and more aerodynamic Discovery still feel willing. It also needs a little more help from the gearbox, espe-cially when towing, though the Defender's gear change is pretty good these days. Unfortunately, Land Rover do ▶

not quote performance figures for Defenders but fuel consumption tells part of the story with the EU combined figure for the hard-working Td5 in a 110 at 26.9mpg compared to 28.3 for a 90 and 30.1 for a Discovery.

responsive Td5

The response of the drive-by-wire throttle on this Defender seemed much more linear than on any other Td5 I have driven. In others on part throttle, there has been a distinct step up in engine response when the pedal has passed a certain point, which was not noticeable in this 9,500 mile old car. It also seemed to pull away with a trailer much more easily, when in the past I have found it surprisingly easy to stall Td5s. Land Rover say there has been no throttle remapping since early examples – maybe I'm just getting used to them.

You are more aware of the Td5 in Defenders than Discoverys and you seemed to be more aware still in the 110, perhaps because there is more floor for the sound to come through. But it has the pleasantly deep, smooth, offbeat grumble that all five-cylinder turbodiesels have, so always sounds good and never suffers anything you could call rattle. The test car had a lack of vibration through the seats and floor at tickover that would have shamed some diesel cars.

Basically, it does not feel out of place in this most luxurious of Defenders. The XS trim level buys you all the factory fit extras available except metallic paint and they are all useful, especially the ABS and traction control package which make a Defender safer and virtually

Above: The length of the 110 makes it a stable tow vehicle. Inset: Second row seats split fold but leave belts on floor. Right: Fascia was improved a while ago, but aircon still looks like an afterthought.

unstickable.

Remote central locking, with an alarm, is also a boon in a five door car where locking the nearside doors is a long hike. The electric front windows mean no more winder handles tapping your leg, being bent double as you try to open a window or having to get out to ask directions – just finger the big switch in the panel in the fascia centre.

Even the black interior's unique part-leather seats are a good idea. The smooth leather is on edges you slide over while the centres you want to grip you are ripstop fabric. The fronts are also heated, which is welcoming on a cold morning though a bit fierce after 10 minutes. The leather trimmed steering wheel and gear knobs are much warmer,

but less clammy, than the plastic (they're now in the Defender accessories brochure with the XS' dark silver radiator grille and head-lamp surrounds).

The front seats are well shaped with good lumbar and shoulder support and, though they are short in the leg, they make up for it by being fairly high. The second row are more comfortably long in the cushion but their flat backs are too low for shoulder support or whiplash protection. Legroom in the second row is good and the rear side-facing seats are fine for adults on short journeys, but the position is too 'knees up' for comfort when all the seats are occupied.

The second row of seats have a 60/40 split fold, with hachback-

style seat back releases by the doors. They fold forwards leaving a long, flat load area with six tie down points, though the seatbelt buckles and their fixings stick out of the floor to damage, or be damaged by, loads.

plush interior

The air-conditioning looks an add-on lump on the lower fascia, stealing a lot of foot space from the front passenger and angling the footwell heater vents at your knees, but it makes a big difference in the summer. It is not linked to the heater so it can't speed up wind-screen demisting, though in the XS that's heated.

Defender fascias were smartened up a while back with more plastic and a central panel housing all the switches as chunky push buttons. The instrument binnacle is all backlit for clarity at night, though you still can't see where the heater sliders are in the dark.

The fascia has much less stowage space than it used to, but the standard cubby between the front seats more than makes up for this with lots of secure covered space and cup holders for oddments needed on the move. You also get map pockets in the backs of the front seats and a net on the rear door in XS only.

If you are going to have a 110 Station Wagon, the XS is worth the extra £3,500 over the County model. After all, the ABS and traction control alone are £1,250 on the County and the total factory-fit goodies bill is more than £4,000, plus the cost of the accessory items, like side bars, dark silver grille and leather steering wheel – and you still won't get the seats. It's

likely an XS will hold its value better than a specced up County, too.

But why would you want a 110 Station Wagon? The only reason I can think of is you need nine seats. If you want the tax advantage in a passenger vehicle, buy the £2,200 cheaper five-seat Double Cab XS and get a more versatile load carrier with no minibus drawbacks. If you want a five-door family car buy a seven seat Discovery. But if you want a Defender choose a 90 XS Station Wagon because that will have all the character of its bigger brother, if not the ride, but be much more fun to drive, more economical and easier to park. **LRM**

Catch the Bus

WHILE THE Defender 90 Station Wagon is legally a car, the 110 Station Wagon is a minibus because it seats more than eight. This means business users can claim back VAT while company car drivers pay a flat rate benefit in kind tax of a few hundred pounds a year, but it has drawbacks.

Anyone who passed their driving test after January 1 1997 is only entitled to drive cars with up to eight seats. To drive a minibus they must be over 21, have held a full licence for two years and have passed a minibus driving test to get licence category D1. With a minibus, that only entitles them to tow trailers of up to 750kg maximum authorised mass (MAM), which is the maximum laden weight set by the manufacturer.

To tow more than that they must take a minibus towing test to get category D1+E and even then may only tow trailers whose MAM is less than the unladen weight of the minibus. Curiously, those who passed before 1997, whose towing ability has never been tested, may tow any weight of trailer with a minibus up to a combined MAM of 12,000kg.

If you have any doubts about entitlement, contact the DVLA whose address is on your licence. Testing is the responsibility of the Driving Standards Agency whose local offices are in the phone book.

URBAN OFF-ROADER

Is the fully-loaded Defender XS just a glorified West End kerb climber or does it have what it takes to survive in the wild?

IT'S THE sort of thing that gets hardcore Land Rover freaks frothing at the mouth: take a Defender, add all the luxury items in the book and then say you are aiming at the more 'urban' user. You end up with a Defender with electric front windows, remote central locking, heated front screen, air conditioning, CD player with four speakers, alloy wheels, heated front seats and leather trimmed steering wheel and gear knobs. But is this a sensible extension of the range or the Defender going soft to appeal to those who think 'green lane' is street running off the A23 in Streatham?

The Defender XS was unveiled at last year's Birmingham Motor Show and is a trim level above County on Station Wagons and 110 Double Cabs. On the Defender 90, the £24,995 XS costs

by
John Henderson

£3,645 more than the County, but adds more than £4,350 worth of goodies. In fact, the only extras left are a sunroof (unnecessary with air con), metallic paint and towing equipment, though there are some things you can't have, like a centre seat instead of a cubby or the off-road tyre options available with steel wheels.

Externally, the only things that pick an XS out from any other

Defender are 'smoked' indicator lenses, which are actually clear, and Brunel finish headlamp surrounds and grille. Brunel is the matt, dark silver metallic finish used on the new Range Rover's grille and gills and is virtually the same colour as the test car's paintwork.

The XS's unique black part-leather seats make the interior look a bit sombre but they do look classy. They are also surprisingly practical because the leather sides give you a hard wearing edge that your bum slides easily over as you climb in, but the centres are a grippy cloth so you don't slide about or get sweaty

Since last year, 90 station wagons have had the bulkhead behind the front seats replaced with a substantial bar which gives the interior a much more roomy feel, and means you can have map pockets on the seatbacks and

allows some heat into the back. More importantly, with the bulkhead there you could not slide the seats to the ends of their runners unless the backs were uncomfortably upright but now you can slide them right back and still have more rake available on the backs. It makes you realise how well shaped the backs are because they offer better lumbar and shoulder support than many taller backed seats. The rear side-facing seat cushions are long for good thigh support.

The leather trimmed steering wheel and gear levers are much more pleasant to use on a cold morning than bare plastic, so you really notice the handbrake's lack of a leather grip. The heated front seats help make up for the Defender's slow to warm heating (a hazard of thermally efficient turbo-diesels). Similarly, the heated front screen keeps it mist free while the heater is warming up as well as being able to rid it of frost in less time than it takes to scrape side windows.

But it's a shame the air conditioning isn't linked to the heater so you could use its extra fan and vents to boost heating or push cooled air out of the screen vents to cool your head more efficiently in summer.

Since last year Defenders have had a new switch panel in the fascia's centre with large push buttons replacing the mix of rocker and twist switches Defenders have collected over the years. It puts all

the switches in easy sight and reach of the driver, so there is no more turning on the hazards when you wanted the heated rear screen. But the air con controls are by your right knee below where the rocker switches used to be.

In the XS, the switch panel is Brunel finish which looks odd because it matches nothing else inside the car, though without it the interior below screen height would be excessively black. The electric window switches are located in the panel and it is surprising how much you miss them when you return to an older Defender. It is so much easier to open either window at the press of a button instead of leaning against the steering wheel

Traction control proved invaluable on the wintry tracks of the East Anglian fenland.

to wind something at calf height. It also means there is no handle to catch on your wellies, but neither is there anything to hook your curry bag on.

The instrument binnacle looks as it has since the 90 and 110 were born, but at night the dials and heater emblems are now backlit for clarity, though the heater sliders are unlit so you still can't see where they are.

A nice touch is that the old scuttle flap levers you pulled sideways to unlock have been replaced with sprung knobs you pull to unlock, making them much easier to use. You lose the fascia's trough of stowage space, but the centre cubby ▶

and seatback map pockets make up for that, and the XS Station Wagons also get a useful net pocket on the back door.

secure loads

Another first across the Defender range this year is load tie-down points for all Station Wagons and hard tops. As most ordinary cars have these, you wonder why it has taken 55 years to get them in an off-roader. They look substantial enough for everyday use but are bolted into the aluminium wheel arches, instead of going through to the steel chassis fixing points, so they might not stand expedition use.

Access to the load area is made easier by the central locking – how often have you leapt out of a Defender to get something out of the back only to have to go back and turn off the engine to get the key? There's no more struggling across to let a passenger in and, because you have a remote sender, there is no keyhole on the passenger door, which is one less

Top: XS has a Brunel finish grille and lamp surround plus nose to house air-con gear. Below: Fascia is smarter than before yet more functional. Below right: Heated part-leather seats plus centre cubby are standard. Below: Look, there's a Td5 engine under that plastic

lock barrel for thieves to pull. If you are carrying something valuable in the back and don't want to risk someone grabbing it at the lights, you can lock the back door manually but, unlike most cars, this doesn't isolate it from the central locking so it unlocks as soon as you centrally unlock.

The XS spec also includes a pair of substantial side runners. These stout bars have a step on them and are strong enough to protect the sills and to allow you to stamp the dirt out of your boots. They are above chassis height so they won't reduce break over angles.

That is the important thing about the XS package, it does not compromise the Defender's basic ability. In fact, having the ABS and traction control package as standard enhances it. The ABS greatly increases safety on- and off-road, especially when towing where

such systems can reduce braking distances by as much as half. The traction control uses the same wheel sensors to compare the rotational speeds of the wheels and, when it finds one turning faster than the others, applies the brake to that wheel. When combined with the locking centre differential it makes it difficult to get a Defender stuck, short of something like grounding the axle.

Even driving it into waterlogged soil with several inches of slushy snow on top never made the Defender miss a beat, with the traction control occasionally 'twanging' as a wheel lost traction. Checking the wheel ruts afterwards revealed the water seeping back over clean tyre tracks.

In most cases you can help it along by easing off the throttle pedal so you are not overriding its efforts, but occasionally, like in really deep stuff, it needs a little more power to give it something to play with. So if one method doesn't work, try the other.

The only thing to get the better of

it was large patches of ice which left the vehicle slowly slithering sideways like any other four-wheel-drive vehicle. This is because the system relies on detecting differences in wheel rotational speeds, so it cannot help if all four wheels are slipping at the same speed, which rarely happens in mud, However, as soon as one wheel finds more grip, it comes to your aid.

lightweight clutch
Every time I try a Defender, the transfer box seems to engage more easily. This one slipped easily in and out of low and readily

engaged the diff lock whether you were moving slowly or parked. Its main box was a little notchy in its long travel between gears but precise through the gates and the clutch has a car-like lightness.

The Td5 engine is inherently smooth, though you are much more aware of it in a Defender than in a Discovery – you can even hear the hum of the centrifugal oil filter spinning down from 15,000 rpm when you switch off. This one was a little less refined than other Defender Td5s I've driven, though it was still not loud enough to affect conversation at high motorway speeds.

The engine had a pleasantly deep note at low speeds which became a turbine hum at around 45mph. By 60mph most of the noise appears to be transmission buzz which starts to sound busy by 70mph, but you'd be shouting in a Defender Tdi by then.

TD5s need more revs than you would expect to pull away cleanly,

Remote control central locking is useful on a car of this size, and there's a useful net pocket on a new rear door trim. Tie-down points stop loads from sliding, but isn't it about time the heater intake was moved to where snow doesn't block it?

especially on deep ground or when towing, but once underway flexibility is good. The torque graph shows a very steep climb from just under 130lb ft at 1000rpm to the peak 221lb ft at 1950rpm and it holds more than 150lb ft from about 1200 to 4000rpm. In a Defender it develops 122bhp at 4200rpm. Land Rover claim an 87mph top speed and European combined fuel consumption figure of 28.2mpg for the 90.

I think one reason some drivers feel it is not gutsy enough is the non-linear action of the drive-by-wire electronic throttle. You get fair performance on part throttle openings but it is as if there is a point of resistance in the pedal and if you push past that, performance beefs up considerably. ▶

WHAT'S IT GOT?

Defender 90XS Station Wagon	
Cost as an extra on County SW	
Part leather seats,	
leather gear knobs and wheel	NA
CD player with four speakers	£150.00
Convenience pack:	
central locking electric windows	£425.00
Cold climate pack:	
heated seats and windscreen	£350.00
Air conditioning	£995.00
ABS/ Electronic Traction Control	£1,250.00
Rear door stowage net	NA
Freestyle alloy wheels and anti-roll bars	£950.00
Brunel grille, headlamp surrounds	
and switch panel	NA
Smoked indicator lenses	NA
Side runners	£239.70
Tinted glass	standard
Cubby box with cupholders	standard
Alarm and immobiliser	standard
Front and rear mudflaps	standard
Heavy duty suspension	standard
Rear step	standard

The pedal seems to need a little more travel than is normal to find the best performance. However, this does make it easier to drive smoothly on rough tracks in high ratio. Engaging low ratio reprogrammes the throttle to become less sensitive which makes it easy to trickle in the power.

Because the 90XS has the Freestyle alloy wheels package, it also gets anti-roll bars front and rear which greatly reduce body roll, but it is difficult to take full advantage of the improvement in handling because the steering feels so remote. In fact, my own aged Defender feels much better on its standard 205R16 tyres with thinner aftermarket anti-roll bars. I suspect this is because the Freestyle wheels come with 235/85R16 tyres which are tall enough to raise ground clearance by 38mm so probably flex more on cornering.

Station Wagons also have heavy duty suspension so ride is firm,

Top: Up to its armpits, yet tyre tracks show wheels never spun. Above left to right: Switch panel is well designed and placed but Brunel finish matches nothing; a stout bar replaces the bulkhead allowing more seat travel and map pockets; XS interior is the best Defender interior yet; binnacle is nicely illuminated but heater sliders are in the dark.

though the long wheel travel means it absorbs larger irregularities better than it does small ones. For what is basically a working off-roader, ride isn't bad even if it is not as supple as a Discovery's.

Does a 90XS make sense?

For £500 less you could have a Discovery S seven seater, but without air con, heated front screen, CD player and centre diff lock, or the character. For some a Discovery would also be too sophisticated for a working vehicle and would lack the 90's extreme off-road agility. An XS is also likely to hold value better than a specced up County.

The XS package is not a softening of the Defender because Land Rover have added nothing that interferes with its central purpose in life. It is all useful stuff that makes the Defender more comfortable, convenient, safer and capable. Frankly, it would be wasted on the urban user, but for someone who has to work from a Defender it will make life a lot easier. **LRM**